THE YALE ARCHITECTURAL JOURNAL

PERSPECTA 36　　　JUXTAPOSITIONS

EDITED BY
MACKY McCLEARY AND
JENNIFER SILBERT

THE MIT PRESS
CAMBRIDGE, MASSACHUSETTS
LONDON, ENGLAND

Perspecta,
The Yale Architectural Journal
is published in the United States of America
by the Yale School of Architecture
and distributed by
The MIT Press
Massachusetts Institute of Technology
Cambridge, Massachusetts 02142
http://mitpress.mit.edu

MIT Press books may be purchased at special
quantity discounts for business or sales
promotional use. For information, please email:
        special_sales@mitpress.mit.edu
or write to:
        Special Sales Department
        The MIT Press
        5 Cambridge Center
        Cambridge, MA 02142

This book was printed and bound
in the Netherlands.

ISBN 0-262-63303-5
ISSN 0079-0958

10 9 8 7 6 5 4 3 2 1

Send editorial correspondence to:
        Perspecta
        Yale School of Architecture
        180 York Street
        New Haven, CT 06520

Faculty advisors
Peggy Deamer and Robert A. M. Stern

Design
Min Choi and Sulki Choi
with initial help from Jena Sher

Printing
Drukkerij Rosbeek BV, Nuth

Binding
Binderij Hexpoor, Boxtel

Contents

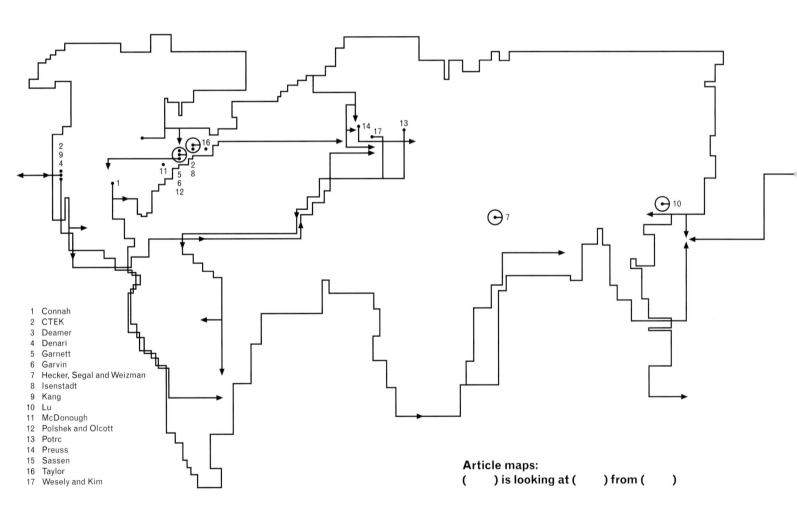

1 Connah
2 CTEK
3 Deamer
4 Denari
5 Garnett
6 Garvin
7 Hecker, Segal and Weizman
8 Isenstadt
9 Kang
10 Lu
11 McDonough
12 Polshek and Olcott
13 Potrc
14 Preuss
15 Sassen
16 Taylor
17 Wesely and Kim

Article maps:
(   ) is looking at (   ) from (   )

The origin of this journal is not far to seek.

George Howe, from the introduction to *Perspecta* 1

Juxtapositions create tension and conflict. It could be argued that our age is characterized by the rapid expansion of formerly binary juxtapositions. In this sense juxtaposition has evolved from an argumentative tool (defining value) into a narrative one (describing existence).

This 36th volume of **Perspecta** begins with the assumption that association is a tool of creativity and of analysis. Our intent is that the juxtapositions (graphic and ideological) in this volume, though created with a great deal of editorial consideration, ultimately subvert that consideration in favor of unforeseen overlap. It is meant as a provocation, a landscape upon which the unexpected can occur.

We would like to thank Cesar Pelli, Fred Koetter and Susie Kim, Marc F. Appleton '72 M.Arch, Jeremy Scott Wood '64 B.A./'70 M.Arch, Hans Baldauf '81 B.A./'88 M.Arch, Elizabeth Lenahan, Robert A. M. Stern '65 M.Arch, and an anonymous donor for their generous contributions.

Thanks to the board of directors of *Perspecta* for giving us the opportunity to make this volume:

Peggy Deamer
Sheila Levrant de Bretteville
Michael Haverland
Gavin MacRae-Gibson
Cesar Pelli
Alan Plattus
Harold Roth
Robert A. M. Stern

Our distinct thanks to Peggy Deamer, who from the start believed in the possibilities; whose intelligence and encouragement was a driving force in the realization of these juxtapositions. Your effort is inspiring and greatly appreciated.

Great thanks to Sulki and Min Choi for so much: speed, understanding, an inspired and stimulating design. This could not have been done without you. Thanks to Jo Frenken for his help in the production of this issue. Thanks also to Jena Sher for noble effort and many hours of interesting conversation. We again thank Sheila de Bretteville and Peggy Deamer for understanding and helping facilitate the production of this journal.

We would like to thank the architects, artists and authors of this issue, whose thoughts and advice were instrumental in the development of the journal.

We thank the MIT press, especially Roger Conover, Lisa Reeve, Laurel Ibey, for (your patience) your great distribution effort.

Jean Sielaff and Jennifer Castelon have been and continue to be central to the education of so many talented people. We thank you for everything.

Thanks to Monica Robinson for tirelessly fundraising.

Many thanks to the Yale School of Architecture, a stimulating environment always in need of great change and always willing to consider changing.

We are grateful to many people for this work, and would finally like to thank those friends that have generously given time, thoughts, ideas, advice, shoulders, ears and help: Aengus OND, Aaron VY, Todd R, Tyler and Liddy, Kate D, Eli H.

The walls are adjourned

FIRST YEAR: THE FICTIONS OF STUDIO DESIGN

PEGGY DEAMER

This is a version of paper presented at the 18th National Conference on the Beginning Design Student, Portland, Oregon, in March 2002.

The first semester of architectural education: such a dilemma. What is the perfect studio program that strikes the right balance between conceptual thinking and formal dexterity? Between material manipulation and cultural critique? Between precedent and innovation? Between sensitivity to site and interrogation of the functional program? Between abstraction and reality? Between large-scale and small-scale? The idea that there must, should be the perfect program that addresses the essential component(s) of architectural thinking haunts many of us who have taught first semester design, whether undergraduate or graduate.

But the possibility of the right program is a myth, and the belief that the program is the essential carrier of a pedagogical position – that it both says what is most important about learning to be an architect and does so straightforwardly – is a fiction. The program indeed says something about what a school or professor thinks is valuable for a student to learn, but it isn't nearly as impor-tant as the entire network of relations – the exchange between critic and student, between student and product, between critic and product – in determining how a student will learn to think and what they will privilege in their design. The corollary of privileging the program as peda-gogical priority is the assumption that the object produced is the proof of success, the goal of the exercise. If we are interested instead in producing an architectural citizen, a person interested in contributing to civic life via her/his skills as an architect, the entire net of relationships of the studio teaching – the critic, the program, the object and the student – needs to be examined.

The critic

From the critic's point of view, pedagogy in the studio is rife with fictions. The work is the students', but as teacher, you can't let anything go wrong. The student's concept is sacred and untouchable – you are merely teaching how best to express that concept – but, you are supposed to ensure that the concept yield a brilliant solution. You are supposed to guarantee that the solution isn't merely formal, but must make sure that the forms are nevertheless hugely seductive. You are supposed to teach that the object produced is more than a direct expression of an idea – it is poetry, not journalism – but insure that every decision made is a logical result of that idea.

The scenario reveals an implicit tension in the relationship between the critic and the student, a tension that, on the critic's side, can feel like a no-win situation: if a project is successful, it is credited to the student; if it fails, the fault is yours. But in sustaining the illusion that she is making her own project, it is the student who loses. A more honest, fruitful, and deeply architectural discussion, acknowledging that the "real" project of the studio very often is not the student's architectural education but the critic's struggle to establish a position in the architectural commu-nity, is displaced. In this scenario, the real "intentions" of the studio can range, for example, from the critic wanting to link investigations in the office with those in the studio to wanting to prove to your dean or chair that you can produce work

Fred Koetter with Shirley Gilat
at the Yale School of Architecture

of a certain sort to wanting to impress colleagues that might come to your final review. While this seems shallow, history not only bares this out, but sanctions it. The modernist model of the studio as atelier, in which the student worked at the hand of the master on projects that very often were real and in the office, made it explicitly clear that not only was the work not the student's but that the intention of this method was ideological combat; that is, the student was being taught how to fight for a position (modernist; avant-gardist; humanist) in the field.

While at the introductory level we have properly abandoned this master script for something much more sympathetic to student individuality, we have nevertheless traded one modernist myth with another perhaps more insidious one: that the studio education is a "pure" laboratory for education that is free of ideological motivation. In moving from one extreme model to the other, not only does the image of the professor remain oddly intact – we can perform magic either in our fascism or our altruism – but it gives the message that education happens in a vacuum. If a studio critic were to state clearly what role the studio played in his or her own practice, it would encourage students to understand that their stake in the studio was not only their "project" but the manner in which they negotiate and transform – for themselves – the professor's stake in the discipline.

The "development" of the studio – the way you steer the work of the studio – also works under the false illusion that the critic merely implements and makes physical the student's concept. But in fact the critic is determined to make the projects look a certain way (their style; the school's style...). Couple this with a post-modern, post-Greenbergian antipathy for "form" or anything that smacks of formalism and the professor is left with no direct way of speaking about what in fact is directing the design critiques. We as critics will talk about "adhering to the concept" or "articulating the depth and complexity of the intention," but in fact, more often than not, we are asking the students to rethink the forms and their distribution.

It must be admitted that teachers do hold out for that rare project that is not about form; in any case, we all know that form is never an end in itself. But because we are overly fearful of discussing form at all, we make it impossible to explain how it's deployed and what the limit of form's relevance is. In previous periods, it would not have seemed awkward to ask the student to conform to certain formal strategies. Modernism had its strategy; classicism had its strategy; post-modernism had its strategy; decon had its strategy (although we didn't talk about it). But our current dislike for thinking that we are operating in "stylistic" formal confines allows us to ignore the fact that there is no *tabula rasa* of architectural language. More importantly, we will never be able to transcend the confines of predetermined stylistic agendas if we don't understand the manner in which they operate. Oddly, again, we end up confirming another modernist myth even as we assume that we've moved beyond the first – namely, that the creative process springs freely from our own intuitive and creative process without context, background, or ideological assumptions. It would be better to admit that we

1 ——
In this latter, no distinction is being drawn between those that deal with proportion and those that deal with material or those that deal with a grid and a kit of parts and those that deal with surface. Rather, the distinction is between those that emphasize the teaching of the language of architecture (the syntax) over the ones that emphasize the use to which this is going to be put (semantics, or the "program" in the traditional sense).

are talking about form and, much more scarily, style, when we push the project around. In that way we will be able to lay bare and ultimately put up for review our formalist assumptions.

The program

The program in the beginning design studio is the document that indicates what the critic believes is the most important skill to learn as an architect. If nothing else, you must learn.... abstraction; to see the world for what it really is; organization and hierarchy; environmental harmony; that architecture is essentially urban, or technical, or material, or environmental; that it establishes a philosophical position about being in the world; that it works in relationship to the body....

Regardless of whether the stated program is to make a viewing device to analyze a site or to start your design process by using planes and sticks, or light, or examining a brick, the point is not that any of these are the best activity, but rather that any or all will teach the student to attack a problem with a certain set of contrivances foregrounding not the solution, but the poetic tropes applied to the solution, contrivances that are essential, even if not *a priori*, universal or constant – to telling a persuasive story. The implications of this are two-fold: 1) the exact program is less essential than the contrivances it assumes; and 2) the role of form and aesthetics cannot be overlooked. No matter how smart a student's concept is, if it isn't visually appealing, no one will pay attention. To say this doesn't propose being shallow; it proposes being honest.

The theorems of the Russian Formalists are relevant here. The Russian Formalists believed that in contrast to everyday language, the point of which is to communicate efficiently, poetic speech/writing roughens language and forces the listener/reader to feel the difficult syllable and unfamiliar syntax. This process, defamiliarization, was seen to bring language to life, waking it from the slumber of overuse and habit. Essential to this defamiliarization was what Viktor Shklovsky called the laying bare of technique or exposure of devices, the overt exposure of the maker's/author's manipulation of the object. The distinction was drawn between "story" (what happens) and "plot" (the fashioning of the telling of the story by artificial interruption and digression). The relevant phenomena here are the fact that the artificiality of the devices as well as the self-conscious presentation of the authorial manipulation becomes not the problem but the success of an artistic piece.

Most first semester programs can be divided between those that emphasize the need to tell a story and those that emphasize plot. The first are those that privilege function and/or concept, the second that push form and poetic license.[1] The strongest are those that understand the interplay and acknowledge that a story without persuasiveness or persuasiveness without a story are equally shallow. In any case, the specifics of the written program matter less than the opportunity to experience this duality.

Russian Formalism, the notion of defamiliarization, and an acknowledgement of the role of devices falls into a larger examination of formalism. The negative connotation associated with formalism is a result, in the art world in general, of our reaction to a type of Anglo-Saxon criticism that comes down to us from the work of Roger Fry and Clive Bell and, more recently, Clement Greenberg. This tradition emphasizes composition as the cornerstone of formalism and has been associated with a trivialization of the meaning and value of a work of art. Its equally disparaged corollary in architecture is the peda-gogical tradition associated with the French architect-teacher Durand in which architecture was taught as a series of compositional strategies that were organized by the use of graph paper and the identification of certain organizational principles underlying all buildings, past, present and future.

Buildings were identified by their component plan parts – entrance, atrium, vestibule, passage – or component façade elements – windows, entrance, arches, etc. – and laid out, with the use of the graph paper, according to a particular relational strategies. The criticism here was/is not only that the meaning of the building is ignored, but also that the relational options are presented as universal and comprehensive.

A more updated version of this Franco/Anglo-Saxon formalist tradition is the work of Ching. Ching, as we know, wrote a book that tells us about architectural composition, from the elements of architecture – point, line, plane, etc. – to the principles of ordering – axis, symmetry, hierarchy, rhythm/repetition, datum, transformation. Ching identifies issues that are much more compre-hensive and open-ended than Durand, but for argument's sake, the point is that he, like Durand, is understood to limit our notion of architecture to a list of overly confined elements and formal strategies that both precludes options and implies a formula approach to design.

In this tradition must be placed the nine-square grid problem given out by Cooper Union in the '60s and '70s, in which students were asked to locate predetermined elements into a grid to discover the means of controlling space.

There are many wonderful things about the nine-square grid problem that overcomes the problems of Durand and Ching – it doesn't tell us what operations to make and it doesn't imply that adhering to certain operational strategies guaran-tees anything meaningful, valuable or persuasive.[2] But still, the point is that this Franco/Anglo-Saxon notion of formalism – that has at its core compo-sitional strategies applied to a kit-of-parts vocabulary – is not where we need to stop if we want to identify formalism as a necessary and perhaps not merely implicit aspect of our teaching.

If one looks beyond this Franco/Anglo-Saxon strain of formalism to ones developed in Germany and Russia in the late nineteenth and early twentieth century, one can discern more fruitful trajectories. Each is different from the other, but more importantly, both are different from the compositional one.

In the German tradition, directly tied to neo-Kantianism (and in line with the thinking of Ernest Cassirer), formalism is not a condition of the object, but one of the subject. The essential issue is how one organizes sensual data in one's head;

the artwork is interesting to the extent that it makes evident the epistemological condition. Composition of the object is not the issue; how our mind organizes and makes sense of the visual material is.

One realm of this neo-Kantian strain of formalism is the idea of empathy: that we project our selves – bodily and emotionally – onto the exterior world. It examines the manner in which we connect to the inanimate world around us and can reproduce this connection in the art and buildings that we create. Again, the "form" is not in the object, it is a mental construct that we bring to the world; analyzing form in this sense is more like psychoanalysis.

Heinrich Wölfflin, the famed German neo-Kantian art historian who categorized five different pairs of opposing ways that artists see and repre-sent the world in changes of style, was the first to suggest that painters see in different ways, and that our task as historians (or subsequent lookers) is to figure out, by looking at paintings or buildings, how the artist saw. The five pairs are: linear and painterly; informal and grand; mass and plane; stasis and movement; near and distant. The first of these are associated with the Classical (Renais-sance) tradition and the second of these pairs are associated with the Baroque. Works of art and architecture were analyzed not to find universal principles of design, but as a way of understanding the visual tropes that different cultures and different artists within them brought to their work. Not only does this attention acknowledge that we visually interpret to the world, it suggests that these modes change with time and culture; they are not universal.

Though Wölfflin's formal method is associated, one, with a Hegelian notion of changes in style and two, a limiting framework for understanding the functional operations of architectural form, in fact the most significant legacy is its proposal that when we look at buildings of the past (or, indeed, the physical world around us) we are not seeing the object as it really is, but rather an abstraction of it, its diagram. Thus the current manifestations of this are, on the one hand, the current interest in diagrams and, on the other, ideas of the gaze as structuring architectural relationships.

—— 2
Also in this tradition are the Deleuzian strategies of folding, since they derive directly – via Peter Eisenman and Greg Lynn – from the same formal tradition of elemental – in this case, surface – operations in a matrix.

N

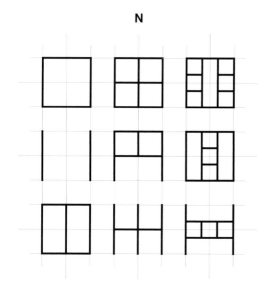

Nine-square compositions, Cooper Union

In the Russian tradition, to return to the beginning, formalism is not equated with the composition of the object or our perception, but, as indicated, the devices used by the author to "defamiliarize" the material; to make the viewer simultaneously aware of the author's manipulation of the object/story (and thereby drawing attention to its author) and its "visibility" (the consequence of its being jarred out of the invisibility of habituation). The concrete material of the work – the words, the sounds, the punctuation and pauses, the physical place in which a sentence finds itself in on the page – was seen as the link between the author's volition and the reader's reception.

A connection between Russian Formalism and the visual arts is made by Vladimir Tatlin, whose work in sculpture explores many of the themes of material toughness, defamiliarization, and laying bare of devices shared by Shklovsky. The uniqueness of his sculptural aim can be seen in a comparison of his 1915 *Corner Relief* with other contemporary approaches to sculpture, in which an ideal, more profound than reality (whether it be the ability to see the inside and outside of a space simultaneously, or the back and the front simultaneously, or to see movement in a static object) is sought.

In contrast to this, Tatlin insisted that sculpture occupies the same space as the viewer, in real quotidian space. To achieve this, the material of the work needed to be foregrounded, not its overall organization. A different notion of form emerges: it is not pressed onto material, but it is the material. The artist brings the characteristic of the material out by exposure and defamiliarization. While this might seem like a straightforward "being honest to the materials" approach, it in fact has much more to do with making the world as we see it unfamiliar via authorial manipulation.

The equivalent to this in contemporary architectural studio projects lies in those projects that analyze an ordinary object and subject it to a series of examinations that make the ordinary extraordinary. The operations that the object is metaphorically put through in these representational analyses make us physically aware of things that we otherwise wouldn't see in the object, for this position, too, awakens modes of visual acuity. It abstracts and reveals the object simultaneously. In both of these latter trajectories, the German and the Russian, the form of the designed object is not formalism's interest; rather, it is the psychological condition of which it is both the cause and the effect. In this, formalism's link to vision is also reframed. Whereas the object-fixated, compositional definition of formalism implies a reliance on the visual-as-empirical, vision in this psycho-epistemological context becomes hermeneutic, not factual. With vision understood as an interpretive device, the formalism is not a register of external "fact" but of inner reactions and projections. The benefit of this is that we avoid the myth of inspiration and the myth of compositional boundaries simultaneously as the student looks for the means to address the written program.

The object

The studio work often operates on the unspoken assumption that the student must pretend that she is presenting a "building" that is either phenomenally there in the room, or will quickly be built after the review is over. This pretense makes it difficult to admit, discuss, and analyze the status of the representation and to show that the only physical embodiment of the project is in the representations; the only life that it will have will be in the 30 minutes of its review presentation and then later in the portfolio. We disdain this fact because there is an assumption that concentrating on presentation is a form of eyewash and deception. But because this disdain cuts off discussion of representation altogether, we miss the point that, for the student, drawings, models, photographs, digital output are not only the only possible analogue to the missing building but the only thing they are really making. In the material sense, the manner in which you treat the paper, the ink, the plaster, the wood, the plexi, the digital out put, indicates the respect that will be shown for the buildings they will eventually design. Moreover, in the organizational sense, the manner in which you understand the space of the room in which the presentation occurs determines the audience's physical relationship to the project; controlling the sequencing of your allotted presentation time indicates your grasp of space as a social construct. Again, the aim isn't to fetishize the presentation as much as to see it as the actual physical artifact in your control.

The implicit belief in the "missing" building also avoids a discussion of what status the actual building, as opposed to its representation, has in architectural discourse. The nostalgic belief that the only authentic experience of architecture is the building itself leaves the students of architecture with the odd message that if they haven't been to all the buildings they are learning about, they are getting a pseudo-education. Relying as it does on texts, magazines, and slides, architectural pedagogy has to embrace the critical issue of photographic representation, not shun it. We should not fear the production of images; rather,

Vladimir Tatlin, *Corner Relief*, 1915

we should analyze, learn about and control its methods. Even as Loos spurned the photographing of his projects, he was a master of the photograph's dissemination, insuring that they enter cultural discourse not on the level of eyewash but as critique.

The following are some projects from different schools and different eras that are interesting for their acknowledgment of the difficult status of the architectural objects that we ask the students to make. Not all are first year, but they could be.

In the first projects, *A Bridge for Contemplation* (Sam Anderson, Cooper Union) and *Medieval Interpretation* (Leslie Gill, Cooper Union), the objects are multi-scaled; they address the body in both representational scale and real scale. The model of the bridge – a draw-bridge that is carefully analyzed for imagined structural loads – represents a "real" bridge, the members, cables,

planks at appropriate representation scale, while also calling attention to the fact that the "wall," described as a fifth floor brick wall of a dance studio, is nothing other than a block of wood that pretends to be nothing other than what it is. Balance, counter weight, suspension, stability, stasis is not just pointed to by representational gestures but is physically present, in the model itself; we are viscerally engaged in these principles. In the medieval studies, where the pictorial principle of medieval painting – using scale and size flexibly to indicate importance, not relative distance or actual size – is used to portray buildings/landscapes of ambiguous scale and index while the idiosyncrasies of the materials of model itself become as well a primary point of aesthetic reference. In both, abstraction is born of the dual play of representation and objecthood, analogue and fact.

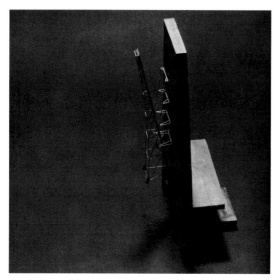

Sam Anderson, *A Bridge for Contemplation*, Cooper Union

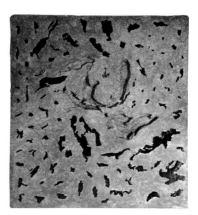

Leslie Gill, *Medieval Interpretation*, Cooper Union

The Question Concerning Technology: The Rise or Fall of CTEK

In many ways our survival is predicated on our diverse penetration of industries, which also provides a sense of credibility
— Tammy Edmonds

CTEK is a high technology company dealing with fabrication and the realization of complex architectural projects. CTEK architectural division was created when Frank Gehry approached them to fabricate the compound curved glass panels of the Condé Nast Cafeteria in New York. At that time, the tooling and manufacturing process had not been established to accomplish his task, and CTEK, drawing on experience from the aerospace and automotive industries, was successful in developing technique and technology to slump complex compound curved glass.
Since beginning the research and development of this article two years ago, CTEK has been through major changes. At the point of publication, it is unclear what the future of this company

will be. The following conversations are about the direction which architecture is moving, the impact of technology, the necessity for development of new relationships, architecture a successful business model, and inspiration. CTEK is trying carve out a niche in which it can successfully operate as a leader in architectural technology. Success has yet to be determined, but there is much to learn from this company a the questions it asks.

Partial transcript of a meeting with Ruben Suare, Tammy Edmonds, and Jennifer Silbert. Saturday March 27, Starbuck two Tangerine Mochas and one cup of coffee
Jennifer This is part of the problem historically with archite tural technology. You do research with a leap of faith, excite about the design process, and then you don't get the job cor in the end. Because of this, it is critical to be a part of the process — to present yourself as the whole process rather th single end product.

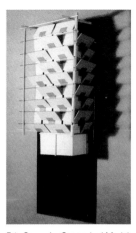

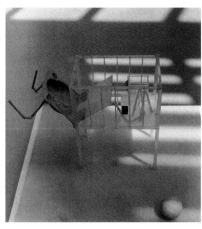

Eric Samuels, *Conceptual Model for Public Bathroom*, Yale School of Architecture

Paul Lubowicki, *Study of Orphanage*, Cooper Union

Daniel Arbelaez, *Window*. Yale School of Architecture

Porta Elmer, Chris King, and Leila Scheu, *Body-Masque*. Cornell University

In the next two projects, a conceptual model for a public bathroom (Eric Samuels, Yale) and the study of an orphanage (Paul Lubowicki, Cooper Union), the ambiguous status of the object – indeed, the fact that the object is an object and not a space – lends an ominous sense to the institutional program, the sense that intimate familiarity with a mechanism reveals unfamiliar things. In the orphanage, the nature of room and objects that fill it, be it the crib that fills/replaces a room or the objects in the crib that displace space and make occupation hazardous, becomes the essential point of analysis. In this, the ambiguous scale of the object, as well as their familiar but unfamiliar function, lends a surreal sense of childhood and its object relations. Likewise, the sense that you, as viewer of the object, provide a third person point of view, is not incidental to the subject-object relationships depicted. The viewer is implicated in the act of containment, affection, and control. In the bathroom, a full-scale analytic model, the focus on the skin of the container as opposed to the activity within, indicates that the primary concern is not the act of relieving yourself, but the difficult, intimate and intimidating relationship that the person inside has with the people outside. At the same time, the tactility of the skin, while activating a visual relationship, displaces it with touch, an indication again that the activity within is primarily tactile, and here displaced to the skin as signifier. In both cases, the body – both that of the actual viewer in the classroom and the implied viewer of the program – is implicated in the act of voyeurism.

In the last two projects, a window (Daniel Arbelaez, Yale) and *Body-Masque* where students were asked to consider the role of sight in interpersonal space (Porta Elmer, Chris King, Leila Scheu, Cornell), full-scale projects identify the self as the site of architecture; the faculty member and student must recognize that studio projects aren't designed in their own ideal conceptual space, but in the self-reflexive environment of the studio proper. In taking on the seemingly innocent act of viewing, both projects objectify sight in the mad object at the same time that they spatialize it, giving meaning only in the specifics of the spatial, body-located context. With the window, viewing is disengaged from seeing, seeing from light passage. Transparency is exchanged for opacity; void for solid. It acknowledges its own

---

Exactly. Fabrication for complex projects requires an [underst]anding of the project that is very time consuming and [cos]tly – research and development. What you just mentioned [is] important, and the process versus the product is what [makes t]he difference here.

You know what happened when I started working for [...] One of my concerns was the company structure – the [combinat]ion of different industries that seemed to drive the entire [busines]s. I did not want to get involved in the politics of the auto-[motive]division, or the aerospace division. I wanted to focus on [archite]cture. Every time we discussed the company it was about [the who]le company, and I would actually stop them – "You are not [going t]o achieve anything this way. You have to focus. Understand [what yo]u have here. You cannot tackle the whole company every [time." W]e are now able to focus on what we do well. Juxtapose [it wit]h a very good understanding of how architects practice, [and I]get something that clicks with the architectural and [constru]ction industries in a new way. And that is the strength that

architects are missing. The industry has segmented itself in a way that architects have become orchestrators.

Tammy There are only a few that are able to penetrate that – to move from draftsmen to a lead power player.

Ruben Even at that level, the most difficult thing about architects is that you are selling your ideas without the strength to implement them. You can look at the material palate of most architects right now, which comes predominantly from catalogues.

Jennifer It's very hard to sell an idea when you have to go someplace else to understand it.

Tammy It's a trust issue as well. The reason that you have this catalogued industry, and I think the reason why architecture has become less exciting, is that you build these relationships with particular manufacturers and you build them because you are limited by your budget, by time, by the scope of what needs to happen, so you rely on the things that you know will deliver. The problem is that the material never really changes. You are just utilizing it in a different capacity. And there are only a handful of

people that can even manipulate the material to make it new.

Ruben Historically, fabrication is done by architects that are pushing the limits of material. People like Alvar Alto.

Jennifer Architects are innovators.

Tammy Years ago architects had the ability to push material limits because the industry was not so segmented. Legally right now we cannot do it. But it must be done. I don't think that I'm speaking here of something that we see as far-fetched.

Ruben When you look at business, you can have a very high-risk business or a very conservative business and everything in between. And CTEK is a very high-risk company. The risks were way too high. We weren't really addressing the very core needs of a corporation, which are very systematic. It was about innovation. It was about creating. Now there is this concrete theoretical base that we can take, address all the administrative issues, and augment it with a clear focus: a picture that you see of a void in the construction and architectural world. We already have a strong technological background. Add the administrative side

weight and objectivity. In *Body-Masque*, one student objectifies furtive glances and makes "a pair of opera glasses for the voyeur;" another studied, through apparati attached to the feet, the nuances of a body which occupies vertical space but sees via the horizon(tal) line; another made an "anti-prosthesis" that puts physical pressure on the face as the different acts of looking and moving are inscribed physically on the body itself. In both of these, sight, itself invisible, is physicalized, spatialized, and culturally decoded.

The student

The student is the final constituent in the matrix, and it is proper to conclude with what, in fact, is the real object of our educational efforts. We are teaching the student to perform, architecturally, in a civilized fashion. At the same time, the student is also the one who functions most fully in the realm of illusion; he or she needs to suspend belief in so many things just to justify the hours put in and the money spent. Tensions between the critic and the student will always exist; trust can only go so far when two people are laying claim to the work and the results. Nevertheless, creating an environment in which the assumptions behind the illusions are discussed can only make the student's critical faculties sharper. It also ensures that the definition of architectural education goes beyond the production of an artifact. We are producing, as identified before, the architectural citizen; we are educating people who will put their design out in the world publicly, with vigilance and intelligence.

There are two things that this means:

1) We, as teachers, need to see ourselves not just as those with knowledge teaching those without knowledge, but as models for how these individuals should engage with the outside world, be it other people, the built landscape or society at large. Education doesn't exist in an idealized space any more than form does; it not only is in the real world, it is the real world.

2) We must be alert to the implications that we are teaching students to tell persuasive stories. We can teach the student how to say things architecturally in a literate if not literary way; but we can't tell them what to say with it. But we don't just make forms, we orchestrate activities, and these activities establish behavior in and positions taken *vis-à-vis* society. When you give a bathroom as a program, you are suggesting that the student take a position about gender and politics of the body; waste and infrastructure; rituals of daily life. When you give a window as a project, you are suggesting that the student take a position regarding the gaze; technologies of mass production versus craft; privacy; the significance of transgressing the boundary of inside and out, individuality and communality. If you give a house or shelter as a program, you are suggesting that the student think about domesticity, gender roles, and family politics; about whether houses precede villages and cities or vice versa. The student will naturally have a subjective and political stake in interpreting that activity and we need to make sure that we don't block access to it.

In describing the potential for the student's story this way, one does not want to invite misinterpretation. To call these concepts stories – as opposed to solutions or the discovery of phenomenological essences (two different claims to truth) – doesn't suggest that these positions are trivial. In the tradition of Richard Rorty (or perhaps poststructuralist thinkers in general), all truth claims – be they historigraphical or philosophical – are nothing more or less than stories. The stories that we tell others and ourselves are indeed how we make sense of the world. Nor does this approach indicate that there are no criteria for success; no criteria for judging that something is better, smarter, or more persuasive than something else. We all will recognize that certain things teach us more about ourselves than we already knew and others waste our time. Again, this is a significant endeavor, and it is ultimately this project that the teaching of architecture at the beginning level aspires to do.

---

and we are well on the way to addressing very strong practical and theoretical needs in the world of building.

Tammy Another irony about this issue is that architects right now want strength. They want that strength. They want the ability to fabricate. Now CTEK can become the catalyst for architects to really grasp the materials and building techniques that they want to use.

Ruben Many companies are extremely focused on material research, and that is a very strong position for architects. If they are able to understand this idea, and if fabricators are able to address their needs, then we are in a fascinating position. The world is changing very quickly to allow for this. Like I said, it's not a far-fetched idea. It is there and we just need to seize it, understand it, and be there when we are needed.

Jennifer Sharing knowledge and research across disciplines was one of the original ideologies of CTEK. I know that you have become more focused on architecture, but will you still have an interdisciplinary center, sharing of information? There always

seemed to be a real richness coming from intertwining automotive and aerospace and architecture.

Ruben This is something that I am not able to grasp very well – the intrinsic need we have to deal directly with these industries and technologies like aerospace and automotive. It is still part of the company, but much less. The impact of focusing on architecture solely and subordinating the development of these technologies is still a question in my mind. The aerospace and automotive industries are still going to be linked because of the material processes, and any time we get a project like the Gagosian sculpture, we have an aerospace person in the office to do consulting and developing.

Jennifer So there is a need for that. It's just whether or not those industries exist within the office itself.

Ruben My theory would be that you have to look to many other industries, such as the medical industry, and research opportunities for innovation, and the specifics of how they are handling technologies. In order to go to the next level we have to look

outside of what we are familiar with.

Tammy I almost think it's better that they are not in the off[...] is a cyclical process. We developed our business structure because of the nature of those industries. When you look a[...] overall funding, aerospace gets the most per dollar fundin[...] their material research and development, which funnels do[...] into automotive, and then traditionally into architectural, wh[...] pulls mainly from automotive for fabrication. This path is th[...] foundation for developing processes. The fact is, CTEK's di[...] fication was the catalyst for other developments, but it was[...] our downfall because we were spread too thin. And the trut[...] that we didn't have a deep understanding of aerospace. We[...] able to functionally make whatever component they needed[...] of whatever material was specified. We started grabbing fr[...] that fabrication technology, but the automotive is truly what[...] were proficient in and were able to use architecturally. Whe[...] started growing we didn't have sufficient resources behind[...] either the architectural or the aerospace divisions, which w[...]

Joy Garnett
Crash
1999
Oil on canvas

THE WALL YOU WILL NEVER KNOW

EVELYN PREUSS

The arresting move, or the modernity of the wall

The fronts of the Second World War had collapsed less than a year before, when Winston Churchill proclaimed, in March 1946, that an "Iron Curtain" had descended upon Eastern Europe, "[f]rom Stettin in the Baltic to Trieste in the Adriatic." His metaphor likened the Eastern part of the continent, and especially its threshold, the German-German border, to a window, a stage or, given the design of movie halls in those days, a movie screen. All of these devices render an object or scene visually accessible but, at the same time, also keep the spectator at bay. The access they seem to grant is a virtual one, since the distance, or screen, that separates the viewer from the viewed impedes her ability to verify what she sees and to become a part of it herself. By casting his metaphorical curtain into iron, Churchill underscored the inaccessibility of the viewed, as his image associates cages, shackles and grids that keep people or animals in place and arrest free movement. This imaginary of the "Iron Curtain" eventually materialized in concrete: the Berlin Wall.

Along the lines of Churchill's rhetoric, which conceived of the spread of communism as the dawning of a new "dark age," the Berlin Wall came to be characterized as anti-modern. Still in 1987, U.S. president Ronald Reagan's speech in front of the Wall portrays the Eastern bloc as regressive, as a slave-driving society that is technologically so backwards it is even unable to feed its people (let alone tend to more consumerist desires), and as a regime that seeks to arrest innate human drives for social and economic advancement. Turning such political catchwords into scholarship, the cultural historian Brian Ladd almost literally quotes the speech another U.S. president, John F. Kennedy, gave in front of the Wall 24 years earlier, theorizing that the German-German border fortification "connoted an attempt, by political fiat, to reverse the growing economic and social mobility of the modern world. The name "Wall," shunned by its builders, called attention to its anachronism and came to signify a crime against history as well as humanity" (19).[1] To curtail movement, to arrest a subject, certainly represents one of the basic functions of walls, but the historical eras and models to which Western politicians and scholars allude do not corroborate their charge that the Berlin Wall constituted an anachronism.

On the contrary, I would like to argue that the Wall emerged as a monument to modernity as much as to the political and cultural imaginary that shaped the second half of the twentieth century and continues to forge the twenty-first. While the Berlin Wall may have resembled ancient or medieval fortifications, it served an entirely different purpose. Whereas the historic structures with which it has been compared – the Great Wall of China, Hadrian's Wall and the Limes – as well as the walls enclosing medieval cities and estates, were primarily built to keep people out, the Berlin Wall was constructed primarily to keep people in. Contrary to the rhetoric of the East German regime that it built an "antifascist protection rampart" against Western imperialism, the troops that guarded the building of the Wall in August 1961 were specifically instructed to prevent escapes from the East. In fact, they were strictly forbidden to fire a shot into the Western direction (Beyer 107). This directionality is also inscribed into the Wall's architecture. Hagen Koch, formerly a cartographer and officer in the East German secret service, points out that the traps along the Wall were not designed to stop

The Berlin Wall

The Israel-Palestinian Separation Wall

— 1
Without explicitly referencing his source, Ladd quotes the speech U.S. president John F. Kennedy gave on June 26, 1963 in front of the West Berlin town hall of Schöneberg: "the wall is [...] as your Mayor [Willy Brandt] has said, an offense not only against history, but also against humanity" (Kennedy).

---

eeding the automotive division. I think now we are at a point to when CTEK started, trying to come up with a ss model that doesn't really exist. Initially, when Eric was ched by Frank Gehry to fabricate this new thing, the was that he had no idea what he was getting into. It was e of that ignorance and bliss, because he didn't really understanding of the whole – like when you are a child see this tree that is so awesome that you just have climb way up, not even thinking about whether it's dangerous. In ays you have that similar opportunity today, where there is essarily a path laid out in front of you. You have to go e path by instinct.

It's interesting the way you look at it. What we do in the tive industry is competition. It's really basic. It's not about ch or finding new ways of doing things. When it comes to cture, what we have been able to achieve has put us in a where the other companies are struggling to catch up. d time again they can't do what we have done so far.

In that sense it is really easy to see that there is so much strength in the development of the architectural division. We are able to capture something that is so needed in the architectural industry, and that is why the projects that we work on are such achievements. And why we get competitors, large companies, just running behind us, trying to catch up. We don't have that in the automotive industry. We don't have that in the aerospace industry. It's very difficult for any company to not address sustainable technologies. What they do good they are going to try and make better. When they need to address something a little different, something that takes testing, it is hard to even get involved.

Jennifer That's part of the appeal of experimental companies. There is a romantic appeal. The challenge is business.

Ruben … and that was one of the failures of CTEK originally. We did not understand what we did best and just focus on that. We did so many things.

Tammy The research takes place in many cases in settings that

are not easily relocated. You have to be in one location, but research is being done by someone else in another location. Information goes to a thousand different places. And really analyzing in detail what we do in aerospace and automotive, I think we have gotten to the point where they are not intrinsic for the development of the architectural technologies. It might actually be the opposite. At the beginning, CTEK was about putting all these people together. You shake them all up and out comes crazy brilliance.

Ruben It has very little to do with any business model. And it's so much romanticized. You have got to be an alcoholic and walk upside down.

Jennifer Extraction is critical because that part of CTEK, the respect and romanticism, is now what allows CTEK to continue past a point of crisis.

Tammy It is important to recognize that. Our fabricators were so entrenched in the automotive. We weren't very good as a management group in making them understand that architecture

traffic from the West, but to prohibit flight from the East (Interview with Hagen Koch in Frauke Sandig and Eric Black's *After the Fall*).[2]

—— 2
See also Flemming.

The direction from which the Berlin rampart was supposed to contain movement makes it more akin to a prison wall than to the ancient and medieval fortifications that were built to protect sedentary modes of production from more mobile ways of staking out a living. Instead of providing protection against the outside, the Berlin Wall primarily served as a carceral enclosure. It was, to use Michel Foucault's characterization of the prison wall, "no longer the wall that surrounds and protects, no longer the wall that stands for power and wealth, but the meticulously sealed wall […] at the very center of the cities" (116). Moreover, the degree of surveillance, regimentation and control that the Berlin Wall enabled by confining East Germans and Eastern Europeans markedly corresponds to the modern prison, which, according to Foucault, epitomizes – rather than negates – modern society (231, 233). As such, the Berlin Wall may have offered more a foretaste of control mechanisms to come than a glimpse into the past.

The fact that mobility is about as old as civilization also points to flaws in Ladd's historiographical model that equates modernity with movement. While he suggests that "in an earlier age, with much less human mobility, rulers would not have needed and subjects would not have noticed this barrier to mobility" (19), the ability to move about has indeed been essential in previous eras – despite a multitude of walls. From the Middle Ages right to the beginning of the twentieth century, craftsmen learned their trade by traveling. For the aristocracy and the upper tier of the bourgeoisie, a grand tour made the man complete. Likewise, students and scholars traveled extensively to study, teach or dispute at various places of learning. And rulers traveled far and wide to stake their claims. Colonial enterprises – from ancient times to the last century – required an immense degree of mobility, moving entire armies and workforces across the globe. Even the American West was still conquered with distinctly pre-modern means of transport, the horse and the buggy (and guns, of course). Forms of government depended on travel, cultures made their living by traveling, and entire peoples' migrations took place without railroads and airplanes. Modernity may have brought with it the invention of more efficient means of mass transportation, but their absence did not prevent people from moving about in previous eras. Certainly, the affordability and types of travel depended on social standing and profession; however, that also has not changed to this day, as Zygmunt Bauman's model of two-tiered globalization suggests: at any time in accounted human history, there have been elites who distinguished themselves from the "lower" ranks of society by their ability to travel. If anything, modern communication and information technology have rendered travel less relevant to governmental tasks and mercantile and scholarly exchange, and, through technological advance, the relative manpower necessary to occupy, subjugate and exploit foreign lands has decreased. In sum, the mobility of previous civilizations may be all the more remarkable given their lack of modern technology, and while technical innovation may have facilitated mobility, it also reduced the need and the incentive for people to get on the move.

Considering the major purpose of walls in previous eras, the correlation between mobility and fortification actually turns out to be the reverse of what Ladd's model posits. It is not because the citizenry grew more itinerant in the modern age that city and estate walls have disappeared, but because

Tammy Edmonds's sketch of core industries

was not a car we were working on, but that you can apply the same techniques. Trying to have that focus trickle down from design to the assembly line, transferring from architecture to automotive…

Ruben There was very little communication between divisions. It was shocking. There is an operations officer in the aerospace division, which is isolated and works well on its own. The automotive division was linked to the operations officers, and an architectural division that was created in response to the project. The architectural division communicates to the operations officer what needs to be done – we speak to him in English and he understands half of it in Chinese and the other half in Japanese. What we got back had nothing to do with anything we spoke of. The architectural projects were not even addressed. We didn't talk about them because there was very little understanding of what we were doing.

Tammy It is very hard for automotive fabricators to transition to architecture. They are used to having an aggressive schedule

moveable assets, by becoming less "real" and tangible, have become less mobile. When exchange value was denoted in precious metals, it could be easily removed from its owners. Since the coins, necklaces and household items that served as currency and as "savings accounts" often were of a generic nature, they could switch hands easily and unaccountedly. They also could be remolded and, thus, retain their value without leaving a trace as to their original owners. As insurance was not commonly available to cover the loss, external fortifications were needed to protect movable assets from unwelcome transfer. This changed with the development of financial instruments to the extent that they replaced movable assets. Since promissory notes, stocks and bills of exchange were of limited transferability, they could no longer be lost in the same way as gold and silver.[3] In addition, derivatives, such as insurance, further assuaged the gravity of financial mishap or risk. With the onset of modern commerce and finance, medieval walls gradually lost their function. While many survived in economically less developed areas, they were frequently demolished in commercial centers, not because they obstructed the mobility of citizens, but mainly for the reason that their sites had turned into prized real estate. By contrast, the security of investments, although of concern for the subsidized Eastern economy, was but a secondary motive for the building the Berlin Wall.[4] As the East German head of party and state, Walter Ulbricht, admitted to his Eastern Bloc peers, the Wall was to serve as a curtailment of East Germans' ability to leave the country westward. In the meeting of Warsaw Pact members on August 3, 1961 in Moscow, Ulbricht justified the building of the Wall by pointing, in particular, to the loss of labor:

> The enemy is trying with all means to exploit the open border between the GDR and West Berlin to undermine our government and its economy, primarily by means of recruiting and trading people. [...] In the interests of the existence and development of the GDR, active measures for ending the recruitment of people from our Republic are necessary. (quoted in Harrison 55; translation by Hope Harrison)

Yet, the Wall was not only designed to prevent the concrete and physical removal of people from the East. The movement that the Wall was to limit was also of a more virtual kind, as in sections where its structures did not adequately obstruct sight, East German authorities put up special screens, called "Sichtblenden," to restrict the view across the East-West border (Hildebrandt 48). By screening out the other side of the border, the builders of the Wall also sought to curtail the agency of the look. After all, seeing is a participatory act that may transcend, even if only to a limited extent, material barriers. As atavistic as the German-German border fortification may have seemed to some, it provided a comprehensive and effective shut-down of exchange between East and West that even took into account contemporary sensibilities of the look.[5]

    The purpose and directionality of the Berlin Wall also distinguishes it from the ramparts of ancient empires and medieval cities and estates in another essential respect, namely the bilateral consent for the delimiting structure. As ancient and medieval walls were built in order to defend the community or feudal household against the "hostile outside," it is inconceivable that the defense architecture was welcomed by prospective attackers and plunderers. In fact, the walls were necessary precisely because marauding groups could not be expected to restrict themselves to a certain demarcation. By contrast, the Berlin Wall would not have been built without the consent of that "hostile

3 — Either they can only retain their validity if properly sold (i.e., they are transferable only with the consent of the owner) or they are registered and thus traceable to their original owner. By themselves, these notes are not worth more than recycling paper, and thus depend for the recognition of their value on the economic entities that issued them in the first place.

4 — While economic factors – apart from the loss of qualified workforce – did not play a key role in the decision to build the Wall (see below), the East German and the Soviet leaderships were highly concerned about Westerners benefiting from subsidized consumer goods and the effects of the disadvantageous exchange rate between the East and West German currencies (e.g., Zubok 24).

5 — This contemporary sensibility is especially expressed in the work of Michel Foucault, whose theoreticization of the look, or gaze, as negotiating power has greatly informed the current preoccupation of media theory with the specular.

---

couldn't switch gears, which posed a budgetary problem. architectural projects don't have the types of budgets hed to them that a concept car does. The industry knows demanding it is to make a concept car. The architectural ct cannot take the overhead of overtime and triple time on ends in order to finish fabrication, and on a cost manage-level it was a very difficult financial constraint because we linked intrinsically to this type of production. You have very high paid automotive managers that had the expertise we needed, but the budget couldn't handle it.

n It goes back to what we said earlier. It's the difference en simply fabricating and being involved in the whole ss. Automotive we got the contract, built the car, done. That othing to do with the process that is followed by architec-offices and construction companies to develop an under-ing of building, aesthetics and material.

ny It's a timeline. In an automotive contract, the moment you e project you are out the hop and everyone gets involved.

Ruben We are now developing architectural projects that won't be built for two years. The projects haven't even been awarded yet and we are designing solutions. Like the air force memorial, they are investing time and energy for the material research and design, and they don't have the project yet. The air force hasn't said, "ok, here's the money, lets go ahead and do it." They have to do the research first to see how much it's going to cost. The design has incredible challenges. The company has to be very flexible. We can't have two hundred employees fulltime. The ability to outsource items and have relationships with people outside of the office is key. And within that are issues of confidentiality.

Tammy It's like a parent watching a child grow. You see the mistakes, and yet you know and understand that those have to be made and learned from in order to mature and become wiser. There was no clear marketing plan or strategy. And it was always very tricky to answer the question "what do you do?" You kind of scratch your head for a moment and stop because there was not

a tight explanation, and I think that now you can say where the business is — its position as a conduit.

Ruben It generates the character of an organization that is sensed immediately by other business. If they know their business well, they will immediately sense that they need you. Otherwise, what are you really doing? You are everywhere, and no place linked to a sense of a business that addresses some need in the world. We need to focus on the company itself, the position of architecture as a business, how they both fit together. How does CTEK operate itself, within itself, so as not to fall into problems of focusing on sustaining technologies. That is not our core business. Our core business is innovation.

Transcript of a conversation between Ruben Suare and Jennifer Silbert, Easter Sunday, CTEK offices, Tustin, CA

Ruben I think that some of the essential elements of this piece have to do with thinking of the architect as a builder, the control that they have. The position of the field right now is such that

outside" – i.e., the Western world – as recent scholarship has shown. Even though the figureheads of both sides, the Soviet premier Nikita Khrushchev and U.S. president John F. Kennedy, professed to liberate the world from imperialist and communist slavery, respectively, both were more concerned with preserving the stability of their own domain than with vanquishing the inimical camp. Given these priorities, both Western and Eastern ideology had been put to a shattering test by the Eastern bloc uprisings of the 1950s. The Eastern leadership invalidated its legitimation of representing the workers when it opened fire on them, and the West's non-intervention in the bloody suppression of the 1953 East German and the 1956 Polish and Hungarian uprisings likewise betrayed its stated intent to roll back communism. As a consequence, the Western leadership came to fear uprisings in the East as much as their Eastern counterparts (Freedman 74–6).

Seen in this light, the Berlin crisis was about more than Allied access rights to an indefensible and economically unviable half of a city: the open border triggered an ideological crisis for both sides and called into question the status quo. Providing an opportunity to escape Eastern prosecution for political defiance, the open border proved conducive to open protest in the East, which, in turn, revealed the Western world's lack of engagement in overcoming the Cold War stalemate. While both German governments adhered to the doctrine of reunification, the breakdown of the post-war division would have destabilized their regimes and, consequently, did not suit their interests. For the West, it harbored the risk that the West German conservatives would lose their power in a pan-German election due to the strong anti-capitalist bias in all of post-war Germany and the poignant arguments the communists leveled against the Adenauer government on account of its Nazi legacy.[6] A re-united Germany with an influential communist party could have meant the loss of Western Germany in military and economic alliances, as a strategic vantage point and as a lucrative market for American, French and British products. The Eastern leaderships likewise were keen on sealing the borders, since the constant flux of emigrants to the West sharply clashed with the proposition of Eastern ideology that socialism would materialize the dream of mankind and provide for the happiness of every individual. Apart from severely draining the East German economy of labor and expertise, the massive loss of skilled workers and intelligentsia also challenged the regime's promise of a bright future brought about by techno-logical progress, which supposedly gained in potential once unleashed from the restraints of profit-oriented calculations, and by the consciousness of workers, which under socialism had advanced to placing the common good before the individual's gain, according to the government's doctrine.

Although – or because – the rhetoric of both East and West built up antagonism and threat, each side needed to remove the tangible reality of the other in order to lend credibility to its self-projections. Thus, both shared a common interest in putting up a screen that would shelter their ideologies from "the real." The ideological double bind, however, prevented both East and West from openly forcing this solution. Only once the Wall had gone up did the East German government claim to have acted in self-defense and reverted to the pre-modern justification for border fortifications by legitimizing the Wall as a protection against Western intrusion. Similarly, ideological considerations obliged the West to refrain from voicing approval straight-forwardly, as Lawrence Freedman points out:

6 ———
East German propaganda greatly exploited both the involvement of Chancellor Konrad Adenauer with industrialists and bankers who had helped Hitler into power and the fact that a staggeringly high number of officials in the West German government had served the Nazi regime in impor-tant functions. A compilation of their biographies was published under the auspices of East German authorities in the 1965 Braunbuch (Nationalrat), which strongly influenced the West German student movement of 1968 (Seltsam).

The conservatives' apprehen-sion of the communists' political momentum is reflected in the 1956 decision by the West German supreme court to ban the communist party (KPD) – and, preemptively, any successor organizations – as unconstitu-tional. The court's reasoning took note of the KPD's impressive election results of the Weimar era, and also had to acknowl-edge the historical parallel of the KPD being outlawed by the Nazi regime twenty-three years earlier (cf. Tschentscher), which in turn supplied the East German communists with evidence of West Germany's quasi-fascist makeup.

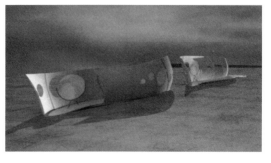

Shell Museum installation, the Netherlands
Left: original rendering
Center: installation view
Right: panel CA crated

The logical solution to the Berlin crisis, one that eventually came about, was to reinforce the division of the city to match that of Germany as a whole. But this was not an outcome that the responsible allied powers – Britain, France, and the United States – could readily embrace, let alone propose […] It was hard to argue for people being forced to live within a closed, communist state. (60)

However, "backdoor diplomacy," intelligence and subtle politicking allowed both sides to reach a consensus regarding the optimal way out of the inconvenient stand-off, or rather: a way to maintain the stand-off by forestalling its dissolution. In fact, Khrushchev may have been inspired by his Washington intelligence when he demanded that the fortification for which the East German leaders had been petitioning him should take the shape of a wall. According to Soviet reports, several officials within the U.S. government, especially the chairman of the foreign relations committee, Senator William Fulbright, and the special assistant to the president, Arthur Schlesinger Jr., had discussed "something like a wall" (Zubok 28). Kennedy also considered a wall a possible solution (Freedman 75), and his noted television address of July 25, 1961, which extended Allied demands only to West Berlin, represented, according to his special assistant for national security affairs, McGeorge Bundy, essentially a green light for closing the border (Harrison 52). Fulbright gave an even more explicit go-ahead in a TV interview, followed by an article in *The New York Times* on August 3, when he declared that the East had every right to close its borders.[7] These statements were made just in time for a conference of the Warsaw Treaty Organization from August 3 to 5, which, as a later CIA report speculated, approved the construction of the Wall.[8] And indeed, Khrushchev and his East German colleague Walter Ulbricht had been eagerly waiting for these signs, as Hope Harrison points out (52–4).

Since the leaderships of both "inside" and "outside" – despite later political gestures – agreed on the Berlin Wall as a demarcation line and, indeed, depended on it for their self-definition, it did not represent a contested space in the same way as ancient or medieval fortifications did.[9] Once again, the Wall emerges as a modern structure rather than an archaic one. Like a prison wall, it reflects a consensus between the "inside" and "outside" governing bodies that enables an inclusion/exclusion stratagem designed to legitimate the hierarchies on both sides. The management of the prison acts as the agent of the governing body beyond its walls by running a social institution that harbors those defined as "unsocial;" and, conversely, the "outside" governing body uses the extraterritorial space of the "unlawful," symbolically contained within the prison, to legitimate itself as representing the law. As the walls of the prison distinguish those who "acknowledge or have the law" from those who "fail or lack the law," they materialize and confirm a binary logic that presents a model for the abundance/lack paradigm, which the Iron Curtain and its concrete successor facilitated and reinforced and on which both Eastern and Western ideologies were based: for "the law," the East substituted "equality" and the West "freedom."[10]

However, prison walls not only act as a demarcation between those assigned with opposing terms, but also as a screen that hides the reality of the "inside" from the "outsiders" and vice versa. In the prison, the inmate loses her individuality and, for the outsider, molds into the generic category of "criminal," because the carceral wall screens out her personal history and her

7 —

Similar public statements were issued by Senator Mike Mansfield, another influential Democrat on the Foreign Relations Committee (Freedman 75).

The reactions of U.S. government officials to the sealing of the Berlin borders on August 13, 1961, likewise reflected at least a tacit approval of the measure. McGeorge Bundy agreed that "it is as well to have it happen early, as their doing and their responsibility" (quoted in Freedman 76; emphasis in the original). Secretary of State Dean Rusk thought the closing of the borders would relax the crisis situation, and President Kennedy went sailing (76).

Two years later, Kennedy presented himself less leisurely in his attitude towards the Wall, when he spoke on a state visit to West Germany and West Berlin. With the Wall having proven itself as an effective and durable screen, he could now assert that "this generation of Germans has earned the right to be free, including the right to unite their families and their nation in lasting peace."

8 —

See "Current" 57.

9

Only the meaning of the Wall was contested: while the West claimed that the Berlin Wall stood for the failure of communism to provide adequately for its citizens, the East maintained that it served to protect the people's achievements against the incursions and sabotage of a capitalism decayed to the degree of desperation. The only standoff in the Wall's 28-year history, the one that, in October 1961, earned Checkpoint Charlie its notoriety, concerned the access rights of U.S. civilian officials to East Berlin and not the institution of the Wall itself. In fact, the Wall was so sacrosanct to the West that it did not even intervene when it stood to lose face over basic humanitarian concerns. When Peter Fechter, an East German who had tried to escape over the Wall in August 1962, bled to death after being shot by an East German border guard, U.S. forces, despite their occupation rights, undertook no effort to rescue the young man over the course of several hours, although he lay within yards of them, crying out for help (Smyser 184).

10

Yet, the double bind of conflicting ideological needs continued to crystallize on the Wall. It confounded the dichotomy to some extent, as the faulty logic of Kennedy's 1963 speech betrays. In order to legitimate the West's concern over Eastern affairs, Kennedy finds, on the one hand, that "[f]reedom is indivisible, and when one man is enslaved, all are not free." On the other hand, he has to claim the West's superiority over the East. For that reason, he resorts to the abundance/lack paradigm and asserts his own freedom in the next paragraph: "as a free man, I take pride in the words 'Ich bin ein Berliner.'" Poignantly, Ronald Reagan repeated Kennedy's lapse when speaking at the Brandenburg Gate on a state visit in 1987, extolling the freedom of the Western world despite his contention that Wall poses "the question of freedom for all of mankind."

---

ects have little understanding of the power of material. is a big difference between a mason builder in medieval and a builder today. There was a deep significance to built then – the significance of material and building. I want to talk about CTEK and say that we will go back to old We are going back to an ideology of building. We are re-ishing the historic position of architecture in a different focusing not only on how you need to build and the sses of building, but also on broad access to the latest ologies.

er One of the things that we have touched on is CTEK as a pe of company. There are new relationships developing en CTEK and the profession of architecture – relationships e not only mutually beneficial, but also with a pointed need k together. Because of legal issues, it is very hard to take responsibility of research and development. So what you s a marriage of two types of companies that becomes a pe of architecture in general – research architecture.

Ruben This is a different business relationship happening, an indistinguishable association where a fabricator plugs into an architectural office. It is technological fabricator and architectural office together. A simple example is when one architect walks in here and sees what we are doing and ten ideas come into her mind. Imagine this relationship established between architects and fabricators, and imagine this exponentially exploding to a whole series of ideas that will change the way we see architecture.

Jennifer So do you think it is about understanding? Clearly architects right now have the power and the tools to design complex shapes.

Ruben To design them.

Jennifer Right, to design them. So we approach the computer and say, "I want a roof that looks like water," and it does become a roof that looks like water, but with little understanding of that thing as a reality. That is the point that architecture is at right now, a lot of schoolwork is digital, but rarely are the tools

available to transition to physical reality. There is a gap in understanding. And it's not only understanding the physical forms, the physical materials but also how it gets built and the pricing and the budget, all of those concerns. So what you have is a necessary fusion. Not only a partnership.

Ruben The ability to understand material – and why would that be a surprising comment. That's exactly what the architects did before. Look at the knowledge that Le Corbusier had about concrete. He was an expert. What will give architecture a huge edge is realizing the difference between then and now. You could become an expert of a specific material in the past. Now your expertise needs to be on what methods are being used to manipulate the materials. You can't just learn about plastics. It's about what is making these things change.

Jennifer In these changes comes the ability to challenge structure and traditional concepts of space. We can talk about the future in a few different ways: one is the actual business model, and the other is about material and changing space.

designs for the future, her face and her body, and prevents her interaction with the "outside." It renders her anonymous, blank, and, by the same token, an ideal surface for projection. Similarly, the Berlin Wall dissimulated "the real" behind it, leaving a void to project upon. Thus, Ronald Reagan, for instance, could paradoxically rely on the Wall's unyielding shielding quality in 1987, when he demanded that the Soviet premier Mikhail Gorbachev "tear down this wall." Without the screen that the Wall provided, it would have been plain for Easterners to see that the "wonderful goods of the Ku'damm [the most exclusive shopping district of West Berlin]," which Reagan unabashedly advertised to them, were also out of reach for most of his fellow Americans, who, after all, lived in a country beset by recession, unemployment and cutbacks in social spending. Indeed, the highest number of applications for emigration to the West came from the southeast of East Germany,[11] where antenna reception for western TV and radio stations was not available. While broadcasts of Western unemployment statistics, news about political scandals and reports on social conditions could have put the chimera of Western freedom into perspective,[12] southeasterners remained undisturbed by these glimpses of West German reality. Thus, they could, to a greater extent than other East Germans, project their own utopia onto the blank that the West represented to them and accept the Western self-acclamation that Reagan so brazenly practiced. The Western self-projection only negated and compensated for the deficits of the Eastern regime to the extent that its own reality remained shielded from view.

This example shows that it was not modern media, but the lack thereof, that provoked people to move. It hints at the fact that modernity is not entirely about movement, as Ladd claims, but also about arrest. First of all, mobility for some does not mean mobility for others:

> For the inhabitants of the first world – the increasingly cosmopolitan, extraterritorial world of global businessmen, global culture managers or global academics, state borders are leveled down, as they are dismantled for the world's commodities, capital and finances. For the inhabitants of the second world, the walls built of immigration controls, of residence laws and of "clean streets" and "zero tolerance" policies, grow taller. (Bauman 89)

Second, even for those belonging to "the first world," mobility, to a great extent, turns out to be an illusion. Although the more mobile elements of society may traverse space, they experience the different locales as one uniform place. The Four Seasons, Hiltons and Holiday Inns, and the travel industry for which they stand, create a more or less generic and exchangeable product, thus minimizing the encounter with the different and foreign (90). With the substitution of local specificity for a new global homogeneity, space becomes ineffectual and virtual and crossing it meaningless. In the same vein, the hybridization of elite culture, to which the travel industry caters, has also not resulted in more diversity, but similarly replaced old, local standards with new, extraterritorial ones. The fact that "[t]he centres of meaning-and-value production are today exterritorial and emancipated from local con-straints" (3) aggravates the loss of spatial meaning. On account of these changes, the ability to overcome space has lost significance. It does not matter that one is in a specific place, when the places have become exchange-able. Thus, the mobility of the consumer age renders the subject, to a certain extent, immobile: wherever she tries to go, the place remains the same.

12 ——
Although East German media certainly covered such topics, they lacked credibility, because Easterners noted their impreg-nation with ideology.

—— **11**
In this area, the per capita rate of people who undertook the excruciating path of petitioning for emigration (which included the loss of one's job, social declassification of the entire family and, potentially, imprison-ment) was about 50 per cent higher than in the rest of East Germany (cf. Leinemann).

Ruben So many questions about our lives will be addressed in the exploration of materials. Property lines are going to be questioned, neighborhoods changed, the rules of cities scruti-nized. I'm a big believer in time, not in the measure of hours and minutes, but in very significant things that happen in life. There are big changes in the world right now. Searching for answers to what is taking place is very difficult, and the future is unclear. The next few years will be really fascinating for the world. I am just struggling to figure this whole thing out. How do we create these relationships? There is no precedent, so the only way of testing is as we go through actual projects, talking to architects and contractors, and trying to see how we fit.

Transcript of a conversation between Ruben Suare, Tammy Edmonds, Macky McCleary and Jennifer Silbert. Citrus Café, Tustin, CA
Jennifer I'll have pancakes, buttermilk pancakes.
Macky I'll have the sandwich. I don't know if I will finish it

though. We'll see.
Waiter How do you want your eggs?
Macky Scrambled. Is that possible?
Waiter Well, how do you usually eat your eggs?
Macky Obviously I don't eat eggs very often. Scrambled, with sausage.
Tammy Belgium waffle with fresh fruit. Strawberries.
Ruben Fruit.
Ruben We just finished a project with Graft Architects – the Tangerine Bar at the Treasure Island Hotel. The architects saw the Gagosian sculpture by Frank Gehry, became enamored with it, and wanted to do something like that. So they basically cut it in half, stood it up, and reshaped in a very similar way for enclosure of sitting areas in the renovation of the new bar in the Treasure Island hotel.
Jennifer They are translucent fiberglass panels that lock together at the sides, lit from above and below.
Ruben That project encapsulates so many issues about this

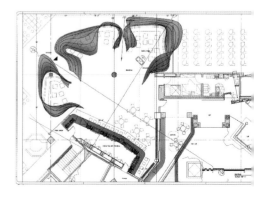

Finally, those who cannot afford the travel industry's products, i.e., those whom Bauman calls "inhabitants of the second world," media offers an equally homogenizing substitute. Their lack of mobility is compensated by the flux of images that are framed according to the ever-same aspect ratio of their television set. With the ease of a click, they can switch between virtual worlds of an ever-same dramaturgy. The only condition for their travel is arrest: to stay put in front of the screen.

In summary, the Berlin Wall was not a measure against the age of globalization, but it served as a prototype – perhaps more visible and tangible – of the "spatial segregation, separation and exclusion" that, according to Bauman, are "[a]n integral part of the globalizing processes" (3). By restricting movement, the Wall immobilized citizens into an audience. Rendering a part of the world inaccessible, it allowed for that unknown to be turned into a projection and to be viewed as the dichotomous Other of a desired self: the Wall closed off the fiction of propaganda from "the real." Functioning like a screen, it turned both East and West into a kind of movie hall.

How the Cold War kept Elton John warm, or why Orientalism sells

Indeed, the Cold War was like a great time at the movies. Enemy encroachment and imminent nuclear carnage revamped the horror genre. A peasant turned world leader who mistook his shoe for a rhetorical device made for good comedy, and summit protocols of twosomes set off twisted – in any case, not entirely straight – romance plots. The Cold War intertwined politics with cultural production, and the appeal and reach of its projections is perhaps best seen in the consumer-driven popular culture of the West.

Elton John's 1985 song and video clip "Nikita," a highly successful example of this pop culture,[13] literally configures the Wall as a convenient divide that provides for the dichotomous projection of self and Other. The Western protagonist, i.e., Elton John himself, is portrayed as highly individual, willful and expressive,[14] whereas the East is imagined as uniform, docile and repressed. As if illustrating the example sentence from *Webster's Encyclopedic Unabridged Dictionary of the English Language*, "Totalitarianism puts fetters upon the imagination" (526), or Ronald Reagan's pronouncement that "[t]he totalitarian world produces backwardness because it does such violence to the spirit, thwarting the human impulse to create, to enjoy, to worship. The totalitarian world finds even symbols of love and of worship an affront," the song characterizes East German border guards – i.e., ordinary citizens serving their mandatory military duty – as "tin soldiers in a row." This conception of the people across the Wall as non-human, lifeless, antiquated toys is visualized as a constant parade-marching drill, which renders the soldiers as mechanical puppets devoid of human feelings and incapable of individual forms of expression. Civilians, similarly, only appear as huddled figures of an indifferent grayish-brownish color, bundled up in winter clothes and hurrying through the background, while, in the foreground, the Westerner sits relaxed in an open car, sporting at first a glaring red sweater and, later, a silk jacket with brightly colored prints. The camera frames the Westerner as a star, as the centerpiece of the display, in frontal medium close-ups, or, as in the night scene, spot-lighted and the sole focus of attention. He stands for the individual who can live out his inclinations and desires unencumbered by any

13 ——
"Nikita" scored a major commercial success with Western audiences. For 18 weeks, the title stayed in the U.S. charts, for four, it ranked in the top ten. In the U.K., "Nikita" became a number one hit, staying for 13 weeks in the charts. In the West German charts, it remained 20 weeks, nine weeks among the top five and three as number one (Domicke). Its success was almost global: in South Africa, for instance, it topped the charts and stayed there for 18 months, becoming Elton John's greatest hit ever there (Samson).

14 ——
Indeed, according to the visual story of the video, his individualism and assertiveness must have swayed the British authorities, which were among the pioneers in the use of video surveillance systems, to let him wear a hat and sunglasses on a passport picture.

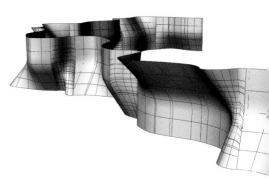

Graft Architects, Tangerine Bar, Los Angeles
Left to right:
original floor plan;
original fiberglass tests using 15' tall interlocking panels;
series of final polycarbonate heat-formed panels;
revised canopy design using 15 compound curved molds;

restraints, while the Easterners remain anonymous and faceless, and appear only in larger groups. Implying that the East is streamlined by a pervasive cult of leadership, the East German woman who Elton John fancies is called after a Soviet politician (rather than Susanne, Peggy or Jacqueline, like her real-life models). By contrast, the Westerner is free to choose even his own name.[15] Singing throughout, he asserts his voice, while the Easterners – including Nikita – have none. Stamped by a homogenizing culture, the Easterner is stuck in her uniform and caged behind a fence, while the Westerner can slip into different roles and identities: he can cross the border – fist-faced guards permitting – change into a different set of designer clothes for every shot and, donning a fez in the last scene, even assume a supposedly more authentic Easternness than Nikita herself represents.

Poignantly illustrating that the Western self-image unfolds in the projection of the Other, Elton John's song addresses, like Ronald Reagan's speech at the Brandenburg Gate, an audience beyond the Wall. While Reagan, in part staging his own importance, explicitly refers "[t]o those listening in East Berlin" and "[t]o those listening throughout Eastern Europe," the video pictures the addressee of Elton John's song as an East German female border guard.[16] However, the song's only line about Nikita in the third person reveals her character to be a fictitious stand-in for any demarcated, and ultimately exchangeable, Other: "Nikita is the other side of any given line in time." In other words, the Other is not genuinely associated with East Germany or the Eastern Bloc, but with whatever is distant and inaccessible enough to serve as a contrasting projection for defining the self.

Consequently, the relationship between self and Other is construed as a contradiction between a loving embrace and the impossibility of the relationship. Reagan's "Although I cannot be with you" follows suit to his "warmest greetings and the good will of the American people;" in the same way, Elton John's friendly invitation, "Just look towards the West and find a friend," accompanies his conviction that "I'll never know how good it feels to hold you." These incongruous constructions necessitate one another, since the imagined affinity is predicated on the distance that forestalls the encounter with "the real" and, thereby, leaves space for projection.

The necessity of a clearly definable divide for the projection of self and Other also transpires in the way both Reagan and Elton John imagine the East/West encounter. Elton John envisions the fulfillment of his relationship to Nikita as dancing, attending soccer games, playing chess and bowling, and, to Reagan, "[i]nternational sports competitions of all kinds" are a matter "close to my heart." Sports contests compare quantifiable performances to determine winners and losers; they do not to develop a common project, bring about a synthesis of contradictory perspectives or foster a sense of reciprocal responsibility, let alone a shared horizon of ideas. The regulated interaction between participants according to strictly defined rules prevents relationships with a dynamic of their own, and the sort of contact it allows does not compromise, but indeed reinscribes, the distance between self and Other.

Elton John's constant photographing of the Eastern protagonist in the video further emphasizes this distance. Objectifying the Other into an image, his photography grants him power, because it confers agency upon the Westerner and renders the East manipulatable, as the final scene of the clip illustrates: through a montage of still images, Elton John makes Nikita smile at him in the same way that Sergei Eisenstein wakes the lion in *Battleship*

15
Born as Reginald Kenneth Dwight, he changed his name to Elton Hercules John in 1972.

16
Except for one line of the refrain, the song refers to Nikita in the second person singular throughout. With questions and command-like structures, the text appears to attempt a dialogue, but fails: Nikita remains silent.

The aural renders a different meaning from the visual, as Nikita is actually a male name, and, of course, evokes one of the Soviet Union's shrewdest leaders, Nikita Khrushchev. The ambivalence of gender may reflect Elton John's struggle with his own sexual orientation at the time, but this problematic is projected onto the Eastern Other, utilizing the stereotype of the feminized East.

industry. So many things are relevant – the lack of understanding right now on many levels in architecture and construction, and regulation of new materials. The complexity in these projects makes people just go crazy. And we got to that point. Because things were submitted to the city that were incorrect, and the city was understandably upset about it. The architects didn't know what to do. Everybody was expecting different things from these panels. Even we didn't quite know how to deal with some of the regulations, but already we have a much clearer picture of what it takes to build something like this, and the consultants we are going to need. This whole process was so informative. The whole time I was pulling out my hair, thinking "somebody just take this thing and make sense of it."

Jennifer Especially on the part of the city of Las Vegas, where the regulations are stringent, and it is often easier to say "no" to experimentation. They are very reluctant to embrace these kinds of things.

Macky Do you think it is a liability issue?

Jennifer Absolutely.

Ruben Definitely.

Macky Beyond that it could be an attitudinal problem within architecture itself. Especially at the regulatory level, where you have people that are not interested in broadening their horizons, and there is real resistance to technology.

Tammy I think it goes back to liability, because ultimately the plan check people put a stamp on the drawings, and it comes back to them. They don't want to take on the liability.

Ruben We had a meeting on exactly this issue. Everybody was trying to speculate on whether this would work. Can we get through? Everybody's response, "I wouldn't sign that if I was the city planner." Meaning, once you sign it's your responsibility. In Las Vegas, they are highly preoccupied with fire issues, so they focus tremendously on resolving that. They will immediately tell you no. They are not going to approve it.

Jennifer This is an interesting project also because the architects, not fully understanding the best tack to take with the

city, tried to pass the panels as walls. By calling them walls instead of art panels or dividers, they were required to pass the fire codes.

Ruben This is where a lot of things can be addressed. Make sure that when we go to the city we have a strategy of how t[h] work. We have to become very knowledgeable about city cod[e] and passing these technologies.

Macky It is yet another opportunity for outsourcing. There i[s] someone who knows how to make it happen. It seems unlike[ly] that an architect or fabricator could do all of these things [as] well.

Ruben It is a general service that CTEK needs tremendously[.] need to have the right contacts and consultants that we can [call] with immediately.

Jennifer Especially now that people are calling on you to do that.

Ruben In our contracts we very specifically state that we ar[e] not responsible for passing city codes. The architects are

Potemkin. Having frozen the East into an image, he literally projects Nikita and her "ten tin soldiers" on the wall, editing the color slides like a film director. Again, the casting, editing and viewing of the image is predicated on a distance between the viewer and viewed and the inability of the viewed to intervene in the process of its manipulation. The fact that the control over the viewed Other implies a disregard for its live dimensions is dissimulated by breathing life into the inert imagery: on his own private wall, the Westerner pictures the Easterner smiling at him in a gesture of affirmation.

In the same vein, the carefully maintained ignorance of the Other is not acknowledged as a shortcoming of the self, but assigned to that unknown itself. Consequently, Elton John perceives a major asymmetry of knowledge between himself and the Easterner. With god-like omniscience, Elton John seems to know exactly how little and cold Nikita's world is: "Hey Nikita is it cold / In your little corner of the world / You could roll around the globe / And never find a warmer soul to know." By contrast, he finds that the Easterner "will never know anything about my home." The six-fold repetition of the line "Nikita, you will never know" highlights the ignorance of the Other as a crucial prerequisite for the projection, and shows how, even within the short length of a pop song, the attribution of self-lack onto the Other becomes a celebrated ritual.

Just as the credibility of the cinematic projection depends on the self-effacement of the cinematic apparatus and technique, the West had to dissimulate its own implication in and benefit from the Wall in order to lend the impression of integrity to its self-image. Thus, the same men who tout their freedom to shape the world according to their own designs not only renounce their political agency, but even their ability to act. The "Nikita" video captures this paradox propounded by Kennedy's and Reagan's asserting their own freedom while ascribing the Wall entirely to the Soviets in the curious ups and downs of Elton John's car window. Rising three times on cue with the words "you will never know" like a semi-transparent, reflecting wall, it illustrates the curious reflexivity of the barrier that creates the Other by preventing unmediated experience and, thus, precluding knowledge. As the window inserts itself between Easterners and Westerners automatically, it also mirrors the failure of Western leaders to acknowledge their political investment in the Wall: the Western protagonist seems unable to control the separation between himself and the Other. Instead, the screen-like window moves – with slight, but telling surrealism – independently of Elton John's apparent intent and actions. Even though he sits in his own car, he is apparently a powerless victim in the face of his own (political) technology – an innocent frustrated in his good intentions to bring love and freedom into the world, a free man unfree.

Yet, "Nikita"'s assignment of lack and abundance along an East/West trajectory overrides this glaring paradox. Exemplifying the image-making made possible by the Wall, it gains its persuasiveness through the strategy of commercial advertisement. The song and the video, relaying the Western self-projection, assert a lack in the prospective customer in order to market the promise of its suture. Accordingly, both Elton John's "Nikita" and Reagan's Brandenburg Gate speech portray Easterners as living little, undistinguished, restricted, cold and unfulfilled lives. In contrast to Easterners' dreary existence, Western identity emerges as a product that will bring about a more complete self. To remedy their lack and attain the colorful, carefree and

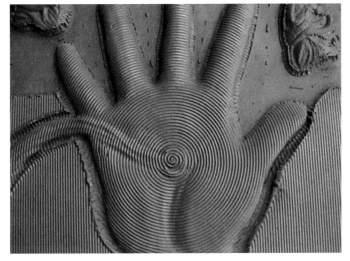

Doors of the Our Lady of Angels Cathedral, Los Angeles
Left: bronze doors sculpted by Robert Graham
Right: hand detail showing CNC milling path

unobstructed individuality that Elton John displays (along with the freedom that Kennedy promises and the consumerist splendor that Reagan hawks), Easterners only need to turn to the West.

Finally, the Wall itself added to the persuasion. By forestalling the verification of the projected images for either side, the Wall imparted them with the finality of "the real." While Easterners could relate the Western depiction of the East to their grievances against their own regimes, they lacked – apart from Western media that reached beyond the border – the basis for a comparison. Hence, they could accept the Western self-projection as a veritable counter-image, a political and consumerist paradise. Similarly, short of familiarity with the benefits of life in the East, Westerners could identify with the models of freedom and individuality their politicians, artists and media proposed, because they inhabited the same side of the Wall and shared with their idols a common Other. And even though they presumably had access to their own reality, it was put in perspective by the Eastern misery that their mainstream media projected. Hence, Westerners perceived their own lives as a little less small, undistinguished, restricted, cold and unfulfilled: like a semi-transparent, reflecting window, the Wall inserted itself between themselves and their experience.

The propensity to self-subversion

In this analysis, the Wall emerges as an effective instrument of power because it limits and channels experience. By the same token, however, it also subverts the mechanisms of power it helps to keep in place. "Nikita" poignantly illustrates this self-subversion, as the projection dynamic that propelled the song and video's commercial success and, by the same token, the political success of the Western self-image surfaces in the lapses of the video's *mise-en-scène*. Undermining the clip's insistent East/West dichotomy, the houses behind the wall, for instance, feature architectural details such as sash windows, which are prevalent in Great Britain and North America, but not used in East Germany. Thus, the video's *mise-en-scène* associates the inhibited Other with the self. Likewise, the clip shows the Western individualist and the colorless Easterners in the same frame in order to enhance the contrast between them. As a consequence, the supposed Easterners scurry along the wrong side of the wall, and, according to the video's spatial logic, would actually appear to be Westerners. In other words, Elton John produces himself before a background that is just as dreary, grim and cold as the imagined East. And finally, Elton John's projection of Westernness is contradicted by another Western protagonist who is even more faceless, voiceless and undistinguished than the Easterners, namely his chauffeur. He functions as automatically as Elton John's car window and even when he is in the frame, he is almost unseen: his dark, shadowy figure embodies the dissimulation of class difference in Reagan's and Elton John's advertisement of Western society. The lapses reveal the self in the projection of the Other, and betray the eclipse of self-lack in the Western self-projection. After all, Elton John's persona, as the free, brightly colored Westerner against the monotonous, homogeneous mass of supposed Easterners, sells, because it fulfills a need for identification that obviously would not exist if Westerners indeed lived like his character in "Nikita."

---

responsible for stamping drawings and dealing with the city. Architects do this all the time, as a general part of their practice. So they tell us exactly what is needed and we will work to get everything together. In the Las Vegas project, nobody knew who did what when. The president of the hotel asked the architect very pointedly "are you going to get this approved?" and after three weeks something had been done, but it was completely wrong. The letter they submitted speaks about a panel and process that has nothing to do with us. The architects decided that they would submit information from 1997 to see if they could get it through. And the city of course said, "What is this?" And all eyes are on us, because we have done this before, and have an understanding of the process. But in every prior case, the clients took care of all the compliance issues, not us. That is unimportant when everyone is looking to you for answers. **Jennifer** But the truth is, this is also new to CTEK. These panels are not anything that have been done here before. [brunch is served]

Tammy Bon appetite.
The reality is very telling. The ridiculousness of some of these things. Most architects don't really want to go through that level of research. They don't know where to start. They don't have the time or the budgets.
Jennifer This project required more research than we were even able to do, the testing of the panels for fire. Knowing that the city is going to buck up against this technology means you have to be extremely prepared with research and information to pacify a whole line of people. You have to understand how the panels will pass.
Ruben This is an extremely challenging part of this industry, because now what I am finding at a business level is that we have to sell the projects directly to the clients. It's not even the architects anymore. I have to go to the client and describe the projects aesthetically, technically, in relationship to art and architecture. The architects are out of the picture entirely.
Macky In a way it makes sense, because you have the expertise.

It's a lot easier to sell something when you know the produc[t] The problem is to get into the architects mind so that they ha[ve] large enough knowledge of the process not just to present t[he] project to clients, but also to design, to push the limits of wh[at] the capabilities are. In order to do that you have to know wha[t] optimal ends are. This requires an enormous amount of rese[arch] and time, which, as you said, architects don't have.
Tammy It ends up ultimately coming down to a trust issues, w[hich] is why Frank Gehry has such close ties with Permasteelisa, because in the back of his mind he knows that he can rely o[n] them to make possible what he designs. They can't do it them selves, but they can find someone else who can.

The place in the sun: political effect and aftereffects, or how history becomes a wall

The Western self-projection is not just a chimera that boosts sales and approval ratings. Since it is taken as a measure for self-assessment and for the classification of others, it affects the real. In Leander Haussmann and Thomas Brussig's film *Sun Avenue* [Sonnenallee], a teenage love comedy that portrays the East Germany of the 1970s with the benefit of hindsight from 1999, the lead character, Michael, wants to become a pop star in order "to move things," the protagonists' passion for Western pop culture directly leads them to run up against the Wall, and the Box Tops' 1967 hit single "The Letter (Give Me a Ticket for an Aeroplane)" cajoles the entire neighborhood into joining them in a surreal anticipation of the 1989 revolution. In the same way that the film's teenagers admire a friend's belled bell-bottom jeans from a Western department store, appreciate female beauty in terms of Western commercials[17] and counter the limitations of their upbringing with the Rolling Stones' promise of rebellion and freedom, Eastern opposition movements were compelled by the promise of Western affluence and democracy. In light of the West's imagined completeness, they perceived themselves as lacking and focused on the shortcomings of their societies instead of valuing their own achievements. The projections that the Wall made possible eventually brought it down. Taking up Elton John's invitation, "Just turn towards the West and find a friend," Easterners followed Reagan's advice to "tear down this wall," without realizing that it was the premise for their utopia.

As the Wall crumbled, so did the projections it had held in place. The disappearance of the Other is compensated by polarizing the image of the former East much along the same lines along which the Wall had allowed the political regimes of the Cold War to splice and realign identities. One part of this image uses the evidence of pervasive spying, of ruptured careers and destroyed relationships that has been uncovered since the demise of the Eastern bloc to reveal the former East as a dystopia come true. The other part, by contrast, sees the former East as the negation of the deplorable aspects of Westernization, as the Other of the status quo and as a utopia left behind. In this reading, the past turns out to have had everything the present is missing: a social security that deserves the name, the feeling that each individual, even the dissident, has a place in society, is needed and valued and the comity and public safety that derives from a more equal distribution of wealth.[18] Like the Cold War propaganda, both the utopian and dystopian views of the Eastern past are predicated on distance. While the Wall enforced a strict segregation in realms of experience, the new barrier that separates the former East from the contemporary West is time.

It is here that *Sun Avenue*, a rare incident in German post-unification culture in that East German artists secured Western financing for a project with a distinctly East German topic, offers a caesura.[19] Skewing the perception of time, it blends the perspectives of East Germans before and after the Wall into one. Set directly in the shadows of the notorious border fortification, the film acutely depicts the social limitations and political pressures that shaped life in the former East. Yet, informed by post-unification sensibilities,[20] it forgoes the sentiments that hurried the fall of the Wall. Instead, the film renders the East, despite its shortcomings, as a successful challenge to the West: there is no homelessness and no hunger, the prices are stable, people share a sense of community and, deploring Western superficiality in their relationships, they even kiss better than their Western counterparts. Contradicting the cliché of the former East, its inhabitants emerge as the most diverse and individual in the film. By contrast, the Westerners uniformly wear well-groomed hippie haircuts over well-nourished faces and all revel in callously cruel condescension (except for Uncle Heinz who wears a wig and ballyhoos chauvinisms).[21] Cheering on East German police to shoot Easterners, the Westerners overlooking the Wall from observation platforms are a far cry from protesting the Wall à la Kennedy, Reagan and Elton John. As they cherish the border more than the East German border guards, they are implicated in the Wall and the suppression it enables in the East. While the former East is, in every respect, of a perplexing heterogeneity, the West mirrors its own stereotype image of the East.

Despite its pronounced depiction of the East's lack, Sun Alley turns the projection scheme of the Cold War around. In place of the West, the East has become the place where one can be struck with the bliss of abundance without being dowsed in consumerist surplus, where one can assert one's uniqueness in defiance of coercive pressure to uniformity and where one can experience mobility and freedom even in the face of a concrete wall. In keeping with this

17 ——
From Michael's perspective, the film presents the local beauty Miriam in the visual terms of a Western commercial for hair shampoo: her long, blond hair – highlighted in slow motion as she turns her head – flabbergasts the men who watch her entry onto the scene.

21 ——
The only thing that Easterners and Westerners share is an obstinate kind of *naiveté*. The film thus reflects the lack of information, which facilitates the projection of the Other.

—— **18**
In Germany, this reevaluation of the past is a popular phenomenon that misleadingly has been labeled Ostalgie, implying that it involved merely a nostalgia for the past and does not present a hard kernel of criticism in the present regime.

—— **19**
The depiction of the former East entirely depends on Western support, as the post-unification restructuring of the media landscape leaves the Eastern part of the country essentially without resources for supporting an independent film industry.

—— **20**
See Cooke 161 and 165.

message, the film's "overloaded," "over-coded" and "overindulgent" aesthetic[22] belies any sense of Eastern lack. The film's hero, Michael, admittedly a stand-in for the East German filmmakers, comments over the visuals of the empty set (the Eastern side of the Wall, where the main scenes of the film take place) that this was the most wonderful time of his life, and, in interviews, the makers of the film impenitently state that the film was designed to make "Westerners envious that they were not allowed to live in the East" (Hauss-mann 22). In full view of East Germany's detriments, Katharina Thalbach, an actress who left East Germany on account of political pressure during the time depicted in the film, emphasizes on the film's website the "lovely aspects" of life in East Germany, which can be only appreciated now, because the fear that used to be associated with it has gone. As the temporal distance replaces the spatial separation of the Cold War, one's own past becomes an inhabitable place, replacing the West as a utopia.

Yet, by the same token, the former East also becomes as unverifiable as the former West beyond the Wall. "You Forgot the Color Film, Michael," an East German 1974 hit song, abruptly undercuts Michael's reminiscence, and the song's refrain, "Now no one will believe us how beautiful it was here," prompts the camera to pull backwards into the West like Walter Benjamin's Angel of History. The Benjaminian storm blowing from paradise impels the camera to pass through the checkpoint at the Wall and turns the colored image of the East into black and white. The film here reverts to an earlier sequence in which the film lost its color when rendering the point of view of West German and American visitors to the East who find Michael and his friends to be as deprived as "those [boys] we saw in Africa." The Western perspective is the black and white that will prevail. As the camera pulls through the opening of the Wall, it comes to a sudden halt and the screen blackens. Before it would reveal anything about the West, its movement is frozen and the projection collapses. Thus, the film returns to the stage set by Winston Churchill: ten years after the fall of the Wall, it remains a projection screen that arrests citizens into spectators who watch their own failures and insecurities as Other. The brief glimpse of alterity *Sun Avenue* affords ultimately affirms that the Wall, as concrete as it may have been, was a device of the virtual age, allowing politico-economic systems to create and maintain virtual worlds, which divest the political subject of her mobility and her agency, even the mobility and agency of her look.

—— 22
See Cooke 164.

References

Bauman, Zygmunt. *Globalization: The Human Consequences*. Oxford: Polity, 1998.

Benjamin, Walter. "Theses on the Philosophy of History." *Illuminations*. Ed. Hannah Arendt. Trans. Harry Zorn. New York: Schocken, 1968: pp. 253–64.

Beyer, Frank. *Wenn der Wind sich dreht*. Munich: Econ, 2001.

Churchill, Winston. "Sinews of Peace." *Sir Winston Churchill: Speeches* <http://www.winston churchill.org/speeches/sinews.htm>.

Cooke, Paul. "Performing 'Ostalgie': Leander Haussmann's Sonnenallee." *German Life and Letters*. April 2003: pp. 156–67.

"Current Intelligence Weekly Summary, 17 August 1961." Central Intelligence Agency <http://www.cia.gov/csi/books/17240/7-6.pdf>.

Domicke, Dirk. *Charts Service* [http://www.charts service.de].

Eisenstein, Sergei (dir.). *Bronenosets Potyomkin* [Battleship Potemkin]. Goskino: Mosfilm, 1925.

Flemming, Thomas, Koch, Hagen. *Die Berliner Mauer: Geschichte eines politischen Bauwerks*. Berlin: Bebra, 1999.

Foucault, Michel. *Discipline and Punish: The Birth of the Prison*. Trans. Alan Sheridan. New York: Vintage, 1995.

Freedman, Lawrence. *Kennedy's Wars: Berlin, Cuba, Laos, and Vietnam*. New York; Oxford: Oxford University Press, 2000.

Fritsch, Herbert (ed.). *Sonnenallee* <http://www.sonnenallee.de/start.html>.

Harrison, Hope. "Ulbricht and the Concrete 'Rose': New Archival Evidence on the Dynamics of Soviet-East German Relations and the Berlin Crisis, 1958–61." *Woodrow Wilson International Center for Scholars: Cold War International History Project* <http://wwics.si.edu/topics/pubs/ACFB81.pdf>.

Haussmann, Leander. *Sonnenallee*. Boje Buck Produktion, 1999.

Haussmann, Leander (ed.). *Sonnenallee: Das Buch zum Farbfilm*. Berlin: Quadriga, 1999.

Hildebrandt, Rainer. *Es geschah an der Mauer*. Berlin: Haus am Checkpoint Charlie, 2000.

Kennedy, John F. "Remarks in the Rudolph Wilde Platz, West Berlin, June 26, 1963." *U.S. Diplomatic Mission to Germany* <http://www.usembassy.de/usa/etexts/ga5-630626.htm>.

Ladd, Brian. *The Ghosts of Berlin: Confronting German History in the Urban Landscape*. Chicago: University of Chicago Press, 1997.

Leinemann, Susanne. "Bruce Springsteen, Held der Arbeit." *Die Welt* <http://www.welt.de/daten/2002/01/19/0119ku308767.htx>.

Marx, Karl, and Engels, Friedrich. "Die Klassenkämpfe in Frankreich 1848–1850." *Werke*, vol. 7. Berlin: Dietz, 1960: pp. 64–94.

Nationalrat der Nationalen Front des Demokratischen Deutschland, and Dokumentationszentrum der staatlichen Archivverwaltung der DDR (eds.). *Braunbuch: Kriegs- und Naziverbrecher in der Bundesrepublik*. Berlin: Staatsverlag der DDR, 1965.

"Ostdeutschland verliert die Jugend." *Spiegel Online* <http://www.spiegel.de/panorama/0,1518,216416,00.html>.

Ray, Christopher. "Auf ein Wort." *Faktuell* <http://www.faktuell.de/Impressum/EditorialArchiv/e31072000.shtml>.

Reagan, Ronald. "Remarks at the Brandenburg Gate, Berlin, June 12, 1987." *U.S. Diplomatic Mission to Germany* <http://www.usembassy.de/usa/etexts/ga5-870612.htm>.

Samson, John *et al*. "SA Charts 1969–1989." *South Africa's Rock List Website* <http://www.new.co.za/~currin/springbok_top_20_(J).html>.

Sandig, Frauke, and Black, Eric. *After the Fall* [Nach dem Fall]. Umbrella Films; SFB; SR, 1999.

Seltsam. "Tatwaffe Braunbuch." *Junge Welt*. 23 Mar 2002 <http://www.jungewelt.de/2002/03-23/023.php>.

Smyser, William R. *From Yalta to Berlin: The Cold War Struggle over Germany*. New York: St. Martin's Griffin, 1999.

Stam, Robert. *Film Theory*. Malden, Mass.; Oxford: Blackwell, 2000.

Szczypiorski, Andrzej. "Damals starb Europa." *Notizen zum Stand der Dinge*. Trans. Klaus Staemmler. Zurich: Diogenes, 1990: pp. 191–200.

Tschentscher, Axel (ed.). "BverfGE 5, 85: KPD-Verbot." *Deutsches Fallrecht* <http://www.oefre.unibe.ch/law/dfr/bv005085.html>.

U.S. Department of Defense. "Secretary Rumsfeld Briefs at the Foreign Press Center." *Defense Link*. Jan 22, 2003 <http://www.defenselink.mil/news/Jan2003/t01232003_t0122sdfpc.html>.

Wittgenstein, Ludwig. *Tractatus logicophilosophicus: philosophische Untersuchungen*. Ed. Peter Philipp. Leipzig: Reclam, 1990.

Zizek, Slavoj. "You May!" *London Review of Books*, vol. 21, no. 6, Mar 1999 <http://www.lrb.co.uk/v21/n06/zize01_.html>.

Zubok, Vladislav. "Khrushchev and the Berlin Crisis (1958–1962)." *Woodrow Wilson International Center for Scholars: Cold War International History Project* <http://wwics.si.edu/topics/pubs/ACFB7D.pdf>.

RECOVERY/RECLAMATION

WILLIAM McDONOUGH

Cradle to Cradle in the water

1 ——
William McDonough and Michael Braungart, *Cradle to Cradle* (New York: North Point Press, 2002).

Over the past decade, the cradle-to-cradle framework has evolved steadily from theory to practice. In the world of industry it is creating a new conception of materials and material flows. Just as in the natural world, in which one organism's "waste" cycles through an ecosystem to provide nourishment for other living things, cradle-to-cradle materials circulate in closed-loop cycles, providing nutrients for nature or industry. The cradle-to-cradle model recognizes two metabolisms within which materials flow as healthy nutrients.

Cradle to Cradle, the book itself, materially, is a prototype technical nutrient for the publishing industry. It is printed on a synthetic "paper" made from plastic resins and inorganic fillers rather than wood pulp or cotton fiber. The paper is designed to look and feel like top quality paper while also being waterproof and rugged. You can read it in the bathtub – underwater if you like. This "treeless" book is also recyclable – easily so in localities with systems to collect polypropylene – pointing the way toward the day when a book's materials can be used, recycled and used again in cradle-to-cradle cycles.[1]

In early 2003, we worked with Ford Motor Company to introduce a concept car designed to explore safe, beneficial cradle-to-cradle materials. Environmentally healthy materials used in the Model U include Milliken & Co. polyester fabric, a technical nutrient made from chemicals chosen for their human and environmental health qualities, and capable of perpetual recycling. The car top is made from a potential biological nutrient, a corn-based biopolymer from Cargill Dow that can be composted after use. Both are examples of materials designed for cradle-to-cradle life cycles.

This first step toward a cradle-to-cradle vehicle lays the foundation for a clear, long-term vision that sees American automobiles as products of service – customers buy the service of mobility for a defined use period – designed for disassembly, their materials circulating in closed-loop cycles and providing "food" for nature and industry, generation after generation. Ford dubbed the car the Model T for the 21st century.

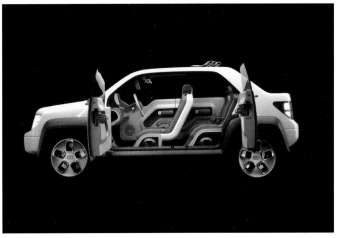

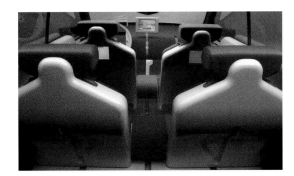

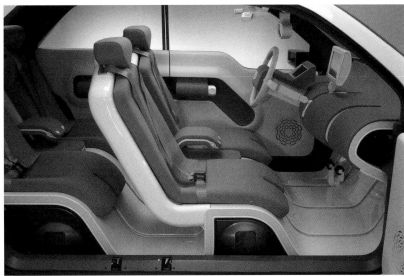

Ford Model U design

PULP ARCHITECTURE

ROGER CONNAH

Pulp Architecture began a parallel life as the Pulp Graduate Studio at the University of Texas in Arlington and the 2003 Brendan Gill lecture at Yale entitled (for obvious reasons) "Pulp Architecture Goes to Yale." At Yale the notion of architecture of a partial destiny, architectural projects or ideas falling short of required and known solutions resonated significantly with students and graduates. When Pulp Architecture was taken to dinner after the Yale Lecture, there was a growing anxiety about the warring ideologies, published manifestos and pretentious theory. Students found much proposed in Pulp Architecture part of their daily thinking about contemporary architecture and, even, life. This was not the usual resistance, tolerated during graduate school only to disappear later. Instead Pulp Architecture met many students from the old Eastern Europe, "Balkania," South East Asia and the Pacific Rim who felt all this depended on life's investment. Pulp Architecture was to meet this Post-Critical situation again and again. The Post-Critical to many is the obvious and inevitable challenge to traditional late-modernist concepts of architecture. Pulp Architecture has begun to go back and forward in time. Pulp Architecture has begun to tap into an urgency that lies outside the usual fame academy in architecture and all the New York / LA stars in and out of Yale and other universities regularly. Also in the air, no longer the feeling of an absurd or futile exercise, there is real enthusiasm for going beyond that "plane of the feasible!" Versions of a trans-programmed, trans-urbanized, transgressed architecture are important but secondary to the urgency for less than total solutions. All this has encouraged Pulp Architecture to continue, attempt something a little more unusual.

Literal flows of data or trash, new urbanism or not, Pulp Architects may not always be architects but they attempt to design from delinquent experiences, in delinquent sites, in delinquent cities. Opting for deferral or an elegant procrastination, they imagine versions of an architecture of partial destinations. But no less relevant, no less resistant, no less revolutionary! Many of these "pulp" practices have one thing in common; they attempt a resistance to an architecture already scripted. The urgency is palpable!

Not a shred of evidence exists in favor of the idea that life is serious. — Brendan Gill

Pulp Architecture is not quite a new architectural program. Pulp is a strategy, an attitude, a parti, a google, an alibi, a motor, an engine, a scroll, a resistance an optimism, a seduction, a fatigue and possibly an ethic... (the list is not closed). If movement itself is essential to our contemporary existence then Pulp Architecture can only ever be a movement-in-progress. Pulp responds to changing social, cultural and economic conditions. Pulp learns mortgage and developmental terminology to appropriate planning inertia. Pulp must even respond to political uncertainty, terror, surveillance politics and deceit. Pulp cannot avoid the new media but it can program its potential uses within architecture. Pulp explores how these conditions and others could re-program architecture. In a contemporary condition "between" rather than "within," Pulp is theory and anti-theory. Pulp is a transportable architecture that seems to wish to stay on the edge. Pulp is trans-urbanism, trans-architecture. Pulp is awkwardness before it is smoothed out. Pulp architecture respects but rejects the star architecture system of individualized spectacles. Pulp challenges existing architecture as much as it challenges architecture already on the edge. Pulp is an architecture informed and fashioned from film, street culture, art, play, terror, surveillance, the hacker ethic, shopping, surveillance, war and new media... Pulp is not only a fiction.

The Professor of Night

"First we take Berlin then we take Manhattan" was scrawled on the remains of a wall in ground zero in New York. There was no time to lose, the future had to be envisioned and the moment taken. Newspaper reviews were ferocious, defeat calculated. Faculty were shocked. How could architecture play such hardball?

"I smell a law suit!" the Professor of Night said.

The Professor of Night was however somewhere else entirely. His apartment in Manhattan had been near Ground Zero but it had survived the attack.

Is this not how architecture in the 20th century was perceived, he thought to himself. Were we not to go forward, tempted by the inventions and ideas of those greater than ourselves?

The last twenty years of the Twentieth Century presented a slightly different version of this. It was ruder, harsher than any of us imagined. Architects played hardball. No one was safe. Students began happily jumping off the shoulders of the giants. Many of them took up living under the armpits of the new giants.

He knew the names of these new giants. He had even had to teach them to the Glazed Hams. Koolhaas, Nouvel, Ito, Holl, Perrault, Herzog, Lynn, Eisenman, MVRDV, Nox, Tschumi, UN, Foreign Office, Rotondi, Denari, Arquitectonica... he could reel off the names like a litany.

The new architecture, he felt, was already in the shadow of the minorities who were on the way to becoming the majority. His old friend Winy Maas from MVRDV, the well-known and well-marketed Dutch team, used a radical diversity and collaborative practice. Though the mix of disciplinary categories allowed these new architects to use experimentation to undo the usual systematic methods, the Professor of Night didn't buy this.

But the glazed hams loved it.

Everyone proceeded as a team today, inviting different and at times unexpected practices to join forces with them. Inside the Academy, there was a growing feeling that all architecture was increasingly about all other architecture. Further, there was a growing feeling that the 20th century was about to be realized in the 21st century.

"This is no longer a paradox beyond any of us," the Professor of Night stated with some aplomb.

The audience stared back. Fire up the barbecue, he laughed to himself recalling a joke doing the electronic rounds during the mad cow disease.

Joy Garnett
Ex Trails
2000
Oil on canvas

The world according to Pulp

Does Pulp exist?
     Yes certainly, there are countless pulp mills mostly on the eastern, forested side of the USA.
     But does it exist in architecture?
     Possibly!
     Is it useful?
     Again, possibly!
     Well, can it explain something in architecture so difficult to explain, the contemporary?
     Impossible, wouldn't even try.
     But if we did, if we attempted one more critical scheme, would it help us be contemporary? And, while we are at it, do we really need another way to be contemporary after all the last century threw up?
     Everything's possible.
     So what would "pulp" be, as a notion? Corresponding to the genre "pulp fiction," would it be lurid, ordinary and excessive? Or excessively ordinary? Would it be something we could relate to a soft fleshy substance, something malleable, the pulpiness of movement?
     Prod it, like a de-stressing palm toy and watch it take another form.
     Any form?
     Or could Pulp be the core of something else brought in from the suburbs of our minds, from the edge, residual, marginal even? Could pulp be an articulated longing, post-ideological, occupying a post-critical space? Might it be a new architectural program, or a strategy, a parti, an alibi, a motor, a resistance, an optimism, an ethic... or could pulp be something that exists merely to avoid being what it already is?
     Outside all, was there nowhere else to go but back inside?
     Certainly we could make a case for this and more. We could see Pulp responding to changing social, cultural and economic conditions. We might even imagine Pulp responding to political uncertainty, terror, surveillance and deceit, shifting the goalposts once more.
     Would this help us out a little? Does it help us know where are we going, if indeed we need to know such a devastating direction as the future?
     We might be braver, or more arrogant.
     Surely if Pulp exists to avoid being what it already is, it cannot avoid all the talk of the New Media? But it might though program its potential uses within an architecture augmenting itself so unhappily. Pulp might be so obvious as to border all ideology with its own barbed wire. And what about the post-critical space, lonely until theorized? Then there's that ugly attractive idea of re-programmed architecture.
     Or do we get more immediate signs, the fresh pulp of architects delivering news flashes, architects running press conferences and architecture about to turn again, whilst the limousines wait down in the street? What about the cowboys and cowboy architecture? Is it useful to follow the *New York Times* style section? Those hand-stitched cowboy boots made not for drafting surely, but for walking from lecture to lecture, 200 times a year? On the road has never been so literal!
     Is this Pulp? Yes, certainly and more.
     To come in at the edge, to resist an architecture already scripted and an architecture to come; are these not attractive notions to the outlaw in us all? But the future: remember what Marguerite Duras said, "If I had the slightest idea about the future, I would still be behaving as though I possessed power."

Googling Pulp

Let us for a moment "google" pulp.
     Pulp is allusive. The immediate resonances are obvious: pulp as in paper, pulp as in cheap, pulp as in lurid content, pulp as in the fictional tradition of the *manga* comic in Japan, or the same-named film *(Pulp Fiction)* by Quentin Tarantino. Pulp is a response to known conditions. It is a response that can either re-emphasize them, make fun of them, or then plays off known conditions to re-order them.
     Pulp re-frames, re-creates, renews.
     Pulp fiction operates this way. Under conditions of known excess, the pulp fiction writer plays up the expected violence and seaminess in the manner of a dirty not magic realism.
     Existing in the conditions of a culture already underground, Pulp is a contra-

Found architectures, from
Atelier Bow Wow, *Made in Tokyo*,
2001

Roller Coaster Building
1: Parachute
2: Sports club
3: Restaurant
4: Entry gate

Super Car School
1: Learners' cars
2: Practice slope
3: Street lights
4: Supermarket
5: Driving school
6: Billboard

Golf Taxi Building
1: Golf driving range
2: Taxi company office
3: Taxi parking
4: Meguro river

strategy. Tarantino's film *Pulp Fiction* invites us to consider the absurdity of a known script. The slight of hand is never so slight, the street never so trivial. Tarantino demonstrated immense skill in re-interpreting what we think is too well known!

Might we not then choose such a fleshy, pithy resonance if we wish to stay away from anything like a new movement in architecture? At the same time might this not introduce us to all the talk of hybrids, crossovers, partial, trans-programmed and software architectures?

Do we do this merely to capture a transition?

Look around!

Everywhere there is, though often hidden to the untrained eye, a new architecture appearing. It is not easily identified. Its position is made uncertain by its own process. The main protagonists may no longer only be architects or students of architecture. This pulpy mass, this informed and unformed architecture, usually acknowledges influence and interference. Carried out by architects, designers, other professionals and students, it acknowledges influence precisely because we know more about previous architecture, styles, histories and critical shapes than ever before. Outside it is there, virtual and real. In cyberspace or in Central Park, in net-works or on the street; we may seek a history in the illusionary spaces that can indeed be traced back to antiquity. But it insinuates and does it well.

Hence pulp!

But surely, you say, there is nothing neat in the fleshy, messy interior, for example, of a pumpkin as it is gouged out during Halloween. And though neatness may not be our objective, it does not lessen our critical responsibility to the present. Publications continue to locate the latest contemporary architects in relation to previous performance, previous signatures. The discourses are controlled by the games played. Where signatures cannot be identified, mutual theory is sought. Branding turns recognizable moves into a community of like-minded designers. Thanks to the Internet we know more about the shapes of contemporary architecture going on in our neighborhood right here, or as far away as Tokyo, Sydney or Alaska. It doesn't really matter where the contemporary takes place, it is accessible and available.

The University of Glazed Hams

Well, look around.

Considering the word "architecture" has been hijacked by software designers, interactive artists, cosmetics adverts, golf course planners, peace negotiators and anti-terrorist war planners, it is probably reasonable to look for something a little wider. The lash architect is on the rebound. I would suggest we see "pulp" in students, in practices, in interdisciplinary teams, in unusual collaborations not only of artists and architects but wider, in research papers and novelists. Yes, in novelists too.

At the university in Texas where I visit faculty speaks good-naturedly about young architecture students as "glazed hams." Well-meant, it is often a symptom of embarrassment and confusion within a changed and changing curriculum. These young students look up, mystified by tectonics and trigonometry, repulsed yet seduced by fashion, fame and 3D Studio Maxx. But as the students start altering the conditions by which they learn each day, do we as faculty miss the point? Life for many of the faculty is always elsewhere. Partial destinies get us there, and partial architecture keeps us there, whilst the "glazed hams" begin to show an increased unwillingness to be content with any banner, any branding.

There is a strong desire in some students to complete their education with more than a little guerrilla strategy. Many in relation to a conventional, often rigorous architectural education, have learnt, been immersed in, and demonstrated their talent in everything the older faculty members have often thrown at them. Many have learnt to clone architecture from the famed and the damned. And many graduates leave school having perfected their talent of producing, what I think we can fairly call a simulacrum of Modernism. We might begin to speak of cloned neo-Modernism.

Much of this is of course highly ordered, cleverly designed, and wonderfully assimilated to some of the latest materials and technological developments. Fostered by the fame academy in architecture, we see a sort of meme machine replicating architectural image from school to school, from discourse to discourse, from city to city. Meme Machine is something we recognize from recent genetic studies, from the work of Richard Dawkins and Susan Blackmore. Remember what Douglas Rushkoff said in his book *Cyberia*:

"May the best meme win!"

Recognizing this, it is possible to observe how many students and graduates in architecture remain unfulfilled. Whilst confirming to some of the miracles of contemporary design and advanced visualization systems, they desire more from an unpredictable, unknown contemporary talent. Many have a further untapped talent to see architecture in a wider, much wider sense, without always knowing how and why this should be put into practice. Their professors, many of them grounded in solid 20th-century thought, pre- or post-modernism, pre- or post-structuralism, believe their time has now come.

I have witnessed this in the University of Glazed Hams in Texas, Stockholm, Prague, Innsbruck, Venice, Tokyo, Graz, Toronto and Helsinki. Combined with added computing skills, new software and advanced CAD modeling, much architecture is seen as a brilliant continuum of the 20th century offering the promise once envisaged in the Modern Architecture movement. There emerges a gospel of restraint. It becomes a battle with the contemporary itself. The result is a significant emergence of what we might call an augmented modernism. For many students though it suggests a replicated, generative process. The replica implies the pulping of the known world.

Architecture becomes a meme machine.

The meme machine

Many new buildings look as if they are versions of an accepted kind of contemporary architecture. The replica is something the public identifies easily, accepts easily, but which invites a continual itch. The glossy publications demonstrate how these buildings perform well to new material, space and function. Like those lifestyle shops peddling all sorts of plastic containers now seen in any city in the world buildings begin to demonstrate their own ubiquitous program. Technological and material sophistication often disguise the generative nature of this architecture. Accepting the nuances that many architects can identify within such new works of architecture, the public however thinks differently. They see versions of architecture always done elsewhere, always down the street from where they live.

This is architecture elsewhere, but not here!

For the professional, the narrow range of representation and spectacle that such architecture holds out begins to look ominous. Advanced visualization programs seduce where previous versions failed. Already the computing software and advanced modeling systems prove able to produce replicated versions of just about any contemporary expression. Interestingly, in my experience, it is often the younger, more talented students and graduates who are being hired in the big architectural practices in Dallas or New York. It is these students who work up projects through the latest 3D modeling software. Their credentials are Form Z, Macromedia Flash, Photoshop, Microstation, 3D Studio Maxx, Director or After Effects.

Where the older convention of drawing, rendering and perspectives no longer suffice, sophisticated digital representations of a previously un-charmed Modernism begin to convince. We see the meme machine at work. It is like a late flowering lust. Versions of Bilbao Guggenheim will not only flow from the consoles of Frank Gehry's office, they will self-adjust and re-appear in any country in the world. Lifted out of the brilliant critical scaffold and agonized parti that an architect like Daniel Libeskind uses to generate his caring "chaosmotic" works, soon every student, every office will be able to enter competitions with "chaosmotic" look-alike shards of agony and memory. The result is a cloned architecture of spectacle and detached representation, rather elegantly represented in Salford Quays Manchester where Michael Wilford (the partner of James Stirling) has produced a somewhat carnivalesque Lowry Building, and across the canal, Libeskind has abstracted air, water and earth into his diagrammatic Imperial War Museum.

Meanwhile there is still something in the air. And it is not debris.

Today we are sensing – if not always seeing – in many young collaborative practices an informed architecture that tries to avoid using the term "architecture." We are sensing hybrids, crossovers in architecture, design and environments. These are not only appearing in books and manifestos about liquid space, portable architecture, trans-architectures or cyber-architecture, they are slowly beginning to establish their own difference from those that closed the 20th Century.

There is also an urgent, possibly political sense that one must resist the architecture that is almost scripted to appear. It is beginning to seem more and more reasonable for the moment to call this process "pulp" and the collection that may never want to emerge, Pulp Architecture.

Sadar in Vuga Arhitekti,
Chamber of Commerce and
Industry, Ljubljana, Slovenia,
1996–2000

Soo Chan (SCDA Architects),
Place for Meditation, Malacca,
Malaysia, 2002

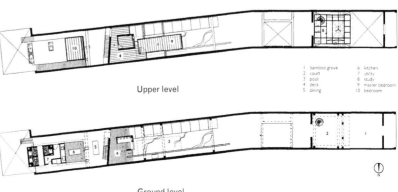

Upper level

Ground level

1 bamboo grove   6 kitchen
2 court   7 utility
3 pool   8 study
4 deck   9 master bedroom
5 dining   10 bedroom

An architecture passing through

We begin to see why there is an attraction to imagine architectures that resist closing too quickly on any critical neatness. "Trans-architectures" is a phrase heard more and more. In the shadow of the architecture of event and event spaces, these new architectures begin to diagram a new inter-personal space. Like the notion of Tele-urbanism from Japan, these might be new forms of urbanism which may ultimately take us onto the next level, as they say, in computer gaming strategy.

In the process of journeying we are always on the way to somewhere else. This is becoming as comfortable as it may be challenging. Students and young design practices speak more and more of partial destinations as if we need not arrive anywhere.

The professors at the University of Glazed Hams look increasingly worried! Are they right?

Should we not be cautious about claiming too much, too quickly for such altered and altering conditions? Certainly! And yet is it not appropriate that we should speak about something like "trans-architecture" that wishes to remain fleshy, juicy, a seductive, soft mass? Are we to stay away from such ideas that have no critical hardness yet? If we are unable to establish difference, if we are wary of announcing a position, should this make our enquiry less valid? Do we need to invent a pulp theory and attitude to do this?

When we think of "pulp" we need also think of the rags, the detritus and the wood that is used to make paper. Soft and shapeless this mass of thinking may be at present, but it will not stand around and await the crushing and beating of less encouraged minds. Whether these are strategies produced simply, accidentally; whether these trans-architectures are the result of easy connections made to incomplete discourses, whether these are environments shaped by more economic means, or whether these are pulped ideas with wilder, uncontrolled vision utilizing huge sums of advertising funds to embed sensational ideas matters little. Instead we are being offered new dynamics and new strategies. We look likely to enter new urban conditions.

In some cases, considering recent work in France or Tokyo, we may already have entered the world of "Trans-urbanism" and "Tele-urbanism." The internet society changes urban conditions, as space itself is colonized by new media. The flow of people, meet the flow of data for example in central Tokyo, in Shibuya. The J-phone, with digital imaging systems built-in, begins to alter the urban space. Community, society, trading and dating, become more than mere urban games. The emergent field that will shape such architecture includes telematics, immersive VR, mixed reality, hypermedia, advanced data imaging systems, telepresence, transgenics, trans-urban generative processes, robotics, technoetics, nanotechnology etc. Life itself is being re-shaped through the architecture of these systems.

But: indistinct or partial as these models of an architecture passing through may be, the forms denied and the forms manipulated from these processes will not prevent these trans-architectures emerging in all cities, in all countries.

The danger of architecture

But is there really "something in the air" outside this usual anxiety and stuttering for the unrevealed? If we rightly sense a resistance to an already scripted architecture, we must surely now consider the conundrum: a movement in progress.

We are all familiar with the term "work-in-progress." When used by a novelist it suggests a draft work. It is always on the way to being completed. It might be one of many draft versions. Or then it might be close to being a final version. In the 1930s Paris when sniffing around James Joyce, Samuel Beckett came up with a strange collection. It was a sort of celebratory volume about Joyce's then work in progress; *Finnegan's Wake*. Beckett of course could not resist punning on the actual process itself. He suggested instability as the very talent and creativity of Joyce's exercise. Beckett called his volume *On Exagmination of a Work in Progress*.

Exagmination is neither the word "examination" nor is it the word we associate with "exacting." Does this not remind us of how a culture like Japan, continually misappropriates the English language and make from it such thrilling hybrids. Or, as William Gibson puts it in his novel *Idoru*, "one of those slogans the Japanese made up in English, the ones that almost seemed to mean something but didn't."

Is this not intriguing; something that seems to mean something but doesn't? In other words, might we suggest this also close to an architecture that almost

Hideki Yoshimatsu and Archipro
Architects, the Cemetery for the
Unknown, Hiroshima, 1998

Njiric & Njiric, Mcdonald's drive-
in, Maribor, Slovenia, 1998–9

Njiric & Njiric, Baumaxx Hyper-
market, Maribor, Slovenia,
1997–8

ecta 36 / Wed, 9 Apr 2003 12:47:14 –0400
the lessons taught in *Learning From Las Vegas* how is
Square indicative of current American urban space and
culture? In Times Square each part is also the whole. The
ibly fragmented nature of the visual space is unified by
arts relationship to time, so that real-time television
scrolling LCD banners and flashing neon lights become
f the same technicolor narrative. But what story is being
re? What does Times Square mean to us now?

C. Taylor / Sunday, April 13, 2003 8:16 PM
Square is to the 1990s what Las Vegas was to the 1980s.
n no more understand the decade of the '80s apart from
than you can understand the decade of the '90s apart
imes Square. When Robert Venturi, Denise Scott Brown and
Izenor turned their attention to Vegas in the late 1960s

and 1970s, they discovered a rapidly growing city, which, they
argued, embodied the emergence of post-war automobile
culture. In the mid-1940s, Vegas was a small desert town of only
4,500 people and by the closing decades of the 20th century, it
was the fastest growing city in the country. As is well known,
Learning from Las Vegas presented a critique of modern architecture, which laid the conceptual foundation for much post-
modern theory, art and architecture. Rather than stripping away
image to expose the purity of structure, Strip architecture layers
signs upon signs until form disappears in image. Though Venturi,
Scott Brown and Izenor could not have known it in the 1960s, the
world they glimpsed in the signs of Vegas foreshadowed the
world of simulacra created by electronic and digital media in the
1980s. To roam the streets of Vegas in the 1980s was more like
being inside a VR chamber than sitting at a drive-in watching a
movie through your car window. The changes in Vegas and its
architecture reflected the pervasive economic changes made
possible by the same technologies that created the media

display on the Strip. A variety of technological, political and
economic developments conspired to create a new form of
financial capitalism in which so-called "real" assets were less
important than financial instruments grounded in nothing other
than themselves.

By the 1990s, this new economic system had spread thought
the world. As markets became wired, a new kind of global
capitalism emerged. The symbol of this new system is NASDAQ,
which was founded after the Depression to monitor trading in
volatile over-the-counter securities. In the early 1970s, it became
the first computerized system for tracking security prices in real
time. It was not until 1991, however, that NASDAQ became a trading
network. Since listing requirements are less stringent on
NASDAQ than the NYSE, most new companies start on NASDAQ.
The capital raised through IPO's and the sale of stock on
NASDAQ financed much of the boom of the 1990s. What is important to note is that there is no trading floor for NASDAQ; indeed,
it is nothing more than a computerized trading network. When

seems to mean something but doesn't, a work-in-progress perhaps. By suggesting a movement in progress however, we accept the idea that this is a movement on the way to becoming a more defined Movement. At the same time we must accept the conundrum once more: the word "movement" is also necessarily in progress.

I think we can now begin to suggest what our new movement in progress might be.

If it is an architecture as a work-in-progress, never quite completed in the conventional sense, is it an architecture soon-to-be-real? Is it a dangerous architecture? According to Sanford Kwinter, Architecture becomes dangerous when it forgoes all that is "pregiven." Gone are the fixed types and predetermined matter. A dangerous architecture, Kwinter continues, takes the actual flow of historical connections as its privileged materiality (not the habitual discrete domains of geometry, masonry, stone and glass), and works these, adapts these through transformations and deformations, in order to engender and bind its form.

A "pulp architecture" then might be a dangerous architecture resisting its own script!

When cool is no longer cool!

Not all Pulp Architecture is of course predicated on the new media and inventive warped space and worm-holing. But all of it will probably be shaped in some way by advances in new media techniques. Architects are naturally involved in this. But the important thing: they may no longer work alone, nor need to, nor indeed want to.

Pulp architecture then would desire to alter the responsibility of the architect. The time for pouring over the journals and surveying the latest star architectural turns is passed. Mongrel, hybrid works of Koolhaas and Holl are only slightly more influential than the re-created modernity and neo-expressionism seen in new computer-enhanced works. Some act out the lost beginnings of the 20th century, others act out the lost ending of the same century.

Today, do we not live in that Pulpiest of all moments, the Karaoke world? According to Malcolm McLaren this is "a world without any particular point of view: where high culture and low culture have their edges blurred. Karaoke is mouthing the words of other people's songs, singing someone else's lyrics. Karaoke is an amateur performance of other people's ideas. It is a virtual replay of something that has happened before. Life by proxy – liberated by hindsight, unencumbered by the messy process of creativity and free from any real responsibility beyond the actual performance."

Remember Malcolm McLaren? Remember the Sex Pistols? Remember the Clash? Should we stay or should we go? Should we rock the Kasbah, or is that not what is happening right now as I write? The clash of civilizations or the clash of fundamentalism; knowledge pinched into hubris, aching for obedience? Architecture primed by redundant ideological warring ready for the perfect fictional take-over?

Pulp architecture then would not be an approach to architecture that believes that it can rescue a type of architecture that might otherwise have gone missing. Pulp architecture would be an attitude that may ultimately have nothing to do with architecture at all! This is hardball time!

NASDAQ launched its trading network, it established an iconic building in the midst of Times Square with a signature electronic sign displaying company logos and stock prices in 16 million shades oft color. But this building has nothing to do with actual trading; rather, it is a broadcast studio for the financial news show Market Watch. At present time, Times Square is bordered by financial institutions with huge signs – to the South, NASDAQ and Reuters, and to the North Lehman Brothers and Morgan Stanley.

In some ways, today's Times Square trumps the architecture of Vegas. Buildings disappear in the play of signs in which circulating images create virtual spaces for flows of images and information. The world Times Square reflects, however, differs significantly from the world of Vegas. In the 1990s, a new finance-entertainment complex transformed the economic, political and cultural landscape. All three major television networks have a presence in Times Square: ABS, which is owned by the Disney Corporation (which has also invested heavily in Times Square), has a broadcast studio in Times Square; the

headquarters of Viacom, which owns CBS, is located at Broadway and 44th Street, and Tom Brokaw regularly signs off NBC's Nightly News with a live shot from One Times Square. In addition to that, MTV and ESPN have broadcast studios in Times Square. Times Square is a critical node where the leading media, entertainment and financial companies dominating the global economy intersect. To trace the lines of this network, it is necessary to decode the signs of Times Square.

P36 / Wed, 4 Jun 2003 15:54:38 -0400
POINT OF PRESENCE (POP): an access point to the Internet. The number of POP's that an Internet Service Provider has is sometimes used as a measure of its size or growth rate. A POP may actually reside in rented space owned by the telecommunications carrier (such as Sprint) to which the ISP is connected. A POP usually includes routers, digital/analog call aggregators, servers, and frequently frame relays or ATM switches.

Your description of Times Square immediately brought to

mind C. G. Jung and his early ideas about the collective unconscious. Can the maelstrom of data and images that is Times Square can be seen as a physical representation (si this unconscious? How can we begin to decode it?

If Times Square is a critical node in this global network also an access point, a point of presence? If so, for whom?

MCT / Fri, 6 Jun 2003 09:17:51 -0400 (EDT)
Yes, there is an intricate relationship between the technolo on display in Times Square and the unconscious. I would, however, hesitate to characterize this relationship as involv physical representation" of the unconscious. Nor would I lin unconscious to Jung's collective unconscious. Rather, I wou extend the notion of the unconscious to Freud and especia Lacan. Elsewhere I have described our psychic experience terms of the technological unconscious. When considering webs in which we are entangled, it is important to realize th information and its processing are not limited to minds or

Hardball time

The last 20 years in architecture has made serious gaming out of language, philosophy and theory. Nothing was believable, when all was believable. The mediation of architecture important for the star architects became a critical act for those following. An architecture opened up to "narrative management" and spin could also be infinitely re-applied, re-appropriated.

This was hardball time.

Fame became more important than ever. Increased pressure on architects to communicate, to write there own press releases for buildings and environments led to a new way of pitching works. It mis-appropriated movements like "Deconstruction" and innovated architecture from it. Controlled suspicion of the star architectural discourses appeared regularly in schools of architecture around the globe.

This was hardball time.

Elsewhere, an unlikely, even untimely utopia for architectural thinking on the fringes of built architecture failed once again to convince. Game strategies were introduced. No fear of theory but no fetish for theory. Theoretical exercises ran up against a structural glass wall. The 20th Century became a repertoire, distanced and distancing itself from its original promise.

This is hardball time.

There is no longer any crisis of influence. Hyper-architecture operating much like hyper-text rejects influence and originality, and slowly begins to widen the site of architecture itself. Ideologies began to weed themselves out. There was no direct relationship to French theory, yet Rhizome was practiced around the world. Now as a website it is considered a social sculpture, more than an electronic field.

This is hardball time.

Pulp architects began to invent their own ways to negotiate this encounter. Creative digitalization arrived and suggested a future hallucinatory architecture. Whilst the star architects continue to design specular and spectacular buildings the pulp architects operate within new menus of radical individuality. Radical pragmatism and public relations exercises ensured an opportunity for partial architectures, architectures without a destination.

This is still hardball time.

Slowly an operative knowledge of architecture began changing, a new vocabulary took over. Notions so beloved in the 20th century began disappearing. In their place, rhizome, sampling, prototyping, nomadism, meme-theory, blur, liminalism, streaming, adjacency, texture mapping; all words like those unhappy mistakes of a Tokyo cooktown restaurant.

This is hardball time.

For pulp architects cycles of dissent and rebellion are secondary to constant invention. Reading is not dead, but it is less on the agenda than electronic cruising. In the popular television game "Who Wants to be a Millionaire?" if you do not know an answer you have a chance "to call a friend." Imagine this is global terms. Using the Net and networks, if you wish to work up and design something, anything, that appears impossible without the help of a specialist or inventor you may – literally – now call a friend, google an expert, date a partner, or fish for a new collaborator. You may even complete the work-in-progress, call it architecture, pulp it – literally – from anywhere in the world.

---

ational machines but are distributed throughout all the ks passing through us. Information processing does not pose consciousness, though consciousness, self-ousness and reason are impossible without it. From neuro-ogic activity and immune systems, to financial and media ks, information is processed apart from any trace of ousness. Moreover, bodies as well as society and culture arily involve information processes. As a result of these lements, it is no longer clear where to draw the line n mind and matter, self and other, human and machine. s distributed throughout the world. In network culture, logy is an indispensable prosthesis through which body nd expand. This relationship is always two-way: as body nd extruded into the world, so world intrudes into body and he networks extruding from and intruding into our bodies nds form the technological unconsciousness. This techno-unconsciousness functions in a manner analogous to s symbolic order by constituting the subject positions

available in any society at any historical moment. Unlike Lacan's symbolic order, however, the technological unconscious is always changing and, therefore, human subjectivity is in constant flux.

Your second question is no less complex. Is Times Square, you ask, an access point, a point of presence? There are paradoxes, perhaps even contradictions, implicit in the definition of point of presence (POP) that you offer, which make your question all the more intriguing. The question concerns the status of presence in the point of presence. First, a general point about the point: The point is never present as such. Rather, it is present only in and through its withdrawing. Every time you think you have identified the point, another point displaces it. The point, therefore, is not present; nor is it precisely absent. Second, and more specifically, the POP involves something like a virtual presence, which is present by not being present as such. A POP, you note, "may actually reside in rented space owned by the telecommunications carrier." This virtual space does not necessarily coincide with the so-called real space. For example,

though its spectacular building in Times Square marks the presence of NASDAQ, the exchange is not there but elsewhere — in a "bank" of computers somewhere in Connecticut.

By suggesting that Times Square is "a critical node where the leading media, entertainment and financial companies dominating the global economy intersect," I want to underscore certain paradoxes. The space of Times Square is both virtual and real. Processes of virtualization do not negate the materiality and specificity of space and place but reconfigure them. Within these networks, some places – both real and virtual – are more important than others. Indeed, it is possible to argue that network culture reinforces the centrality and importance of centers like New York City, London, Frankfurt, Tokyo, Singapore, etc. Within these networks, proximity still has its privileges. Power is access and access is not always virtual.

P36 / Tue, 10 Jun 2003 14:46:17 -0400
In your most recent response, it seems that you are reframing

Images from Jonathan HIll, *The Illegal Architect*, 2000

the discussion to revolve around questions of actuality and virtuality. ("Processes of virtualization do not negate the materiality and specificity of space and place but reconfigure them") This is interesting to us because it is in someway a discussion of being rather than a discussion of thinking or making. In this light can one be critical about the success of the NASDAQ storefront? Is NASDAQ storefront successful as a work of architecture? As a work of theory/criticism? Are there other works that specifically address this issue? Are they successful?

MCT / Date unknown

Your response raises two questions — or two sets of questions: 1. The ontology of information; 2. Storefront as architecture and/or architectural criticism.

If we are to understand the changes now occurring, it is necessary to think beyond traditional oppositions, which would confine information to the domain of the immaterial. As I suggested in my response to your question about the unconscious,

mind is distributed throughout social structures and natural processes. To understand the import of this claim, we must recognize that social and economic processes — as well as physical, chemical and biological process are, in large measure, information processes. Accordingly, it IS necessary to reframe the discussion of actuality and virtuality in terms of being. Information exists not just in minds and machines but also in bodies once deemed material. Information, in other words, is in the world.

It might also be helpful to add a note of clarification about my use of the term "virtuality." It has become customary to contrast the virtual and the real or actuality. From this point of view, the virtual often seems to approximate the possible. This is not what I mean by "virtual." The virtual is neither real nor not real, neither actual nor possible but is the matrix in and through which every such opposition emerges. From this point of view, the virtual is something like what some theorists label the real though it is a non-oppositional real, which is a condition of the

possibility of the opposition between real and not-real.

Second, the question of storefront architecture as it is figured in NASDAQ. I prefer not to use the notion of "storefro this context. Storefront suggests processes of commodifica which, though still operative, are no longer definitive of the economic system. I prefer the notion of screens. What one s in Times Square is an architecture of screens. As I have suggested, to screen means both to show and to hide. It is precisely that play of showing and hiding that is at work eve where today. Yes, these screens are architectural. Indeed, screens increasingly define the space-time in which we dwe Since NASDAQ is not actually a market but is a stage set for shows, there is no opposition between the screens on the ou and the screens on the inside. At the time it was constructed NASDAQ sign showed more than it realized. What is on displ the logos of the sign is the way in which financial markets t selves have become a play of signs in real-time global netw This becomes explicit in Lise Anne Couture and Hani Rashid

Articulated longing or the theory and resistance to everyday life!

Pulp architecture then? From the street up?

In common with street culture, there is a "horizontality" which the young architects and glazed hams take for granted. Inter-disciplinary and collaborative work no longer needs definition. There is not only a thrill in contemporary unrest, there is that licensed accommodation of uncertainty. Take contemporary "hiphop." The main dynamic behind hiphop is sampling. Sampling is a way that pulls beats, bass lines, loops and rhythms, (whole) melodies, even vocals from previously released tracks. The very question as to whether this is a creative, artistic process, or piracy and plagiarism is part of the dynamics involved.

It does not require a huge leap in the imagination to observe that the more architecture looks over its shoulder and sits comfortably with the rise of the media and the pace of trends, "sampling" is a creative, artistic process similar to what architects are now faced with. A technique where recorded sounds or extracts are incorporated into a new recording can be extended to architecture. "Sampling" implies then a technique and vision of incorporating extracts from past and current architecture into new provisional hybrids.

Street culture is model and influence. It has proved more than attractive to shape architecture from the fragments and fusion within other architecture, other disciplines. Old boundaries no longer exist. New attitudes invite new gaming strategies and imaginary soliloquies for architecture. Artistic influence is nothing to be anxious about any more. As Pierre Huyghe said, people, books, images, encounters are all departures for art as well as architecture.

Diagramming and prototyping alter architecture's departure whilst postponing architecture's arrival. Ideas innovate, replicate, loop and fuse. Sampling, transformation, simulation are new tools expanding the site of a practiced architecture. A process whereby things can be changed by rotation or mapping one configuration or expression onto another, "transformation," is not confined to mathematics or linguistics. It offers a set of rules for weaving and transforming the supposed underlying structures of another language into potential architecture. A procedural method which can make a functioning model of another system or process, "simulation" can also function memetically as a diagrammatic alteration, but is itself transformed into an architecture beyond any superficial likeness or imperfect imitation of an "original."

There results a privatization of architectural meaning and a globalization of new ideas. No longer uninhabitable, these are hybrid architectures. The rave dancer has no purpose, no agenda. Software architectures, the hacker ethic and digital engineering have begun re-defining community and privacy, communication and debate. Architecture becomes inter-textual, open to the seductive commerce of influence and exchange.

Is there any such thing as a hostile field in architecture?

From the street up

Pulp practices, like Richard Brautigan in *Trout Fishing in America*, are working on the fringe of praxis itself, continually fraying the edges. Heroes are individual, dangerous and alienating. Buildings representing the sculptural outflow of such heroism are of little interest, though the technology that makes some of them possible is naturally of extreme importance. Pulp is a hunchback strategy. It

Nadim Karam, *Charles Bridge, Prague*, from the book *Voyage*

---

rk Stock Exchange 3D Trading Floor. In this project, the of the market becomes data space through which traders te. In addition to this, real-time market information and rom around the world are both available to investors. The 3DTF is not a storefront but is ScreenSpace.

Wednesday, June 11, 2003 12:18 PM
s ScreenSpace?
aditionally, representations of inhabitable cyberspace from the *Matrix* have widened the temporal/experiential ary between virtual and actual to heighten the experience el. In most cases, however, the qualities of the medium which this travel occurs (the interface) are ignored or layed. Is it necessary for architectural presentations eenSpace to deal with Interface? As a specific example of nSpace, is it important for us to know how one moves to rough the 3DTF?

MCT / Wed, 11 Jun 2003 19:29:04 -0400
ScreenSpace is a term I have coined to suggest the space-time in which we increasingly find ourselves. While imaginative spaces projected in films like the Matrix are suggestive, Screen-Space is not simply an immersive virtual environment. Rather, it is the space in which information circulates to form the environment in which we dwell. In a certain sense, there is nothing that is not interface. I entitled the last chapter of Hiding "Interfacing" to suggest a process that is all encompassing. In thinking about ScreenSpace, it is essential to think beyond information processing machines in the strict sense of the term. Insofar as the body is an information-processing machine, it is an interface. Indeed, the notion of nodular subjectivity suggests that the subject as such is something like an interface for all kinds of intersecting networks. There is no one-way to navigate these networks. While the 3DTF is a "literal" virtual space, Screen-Space is not limited to such technologies. The trading floor of any financial house is ScreenSpace where traders navigate in

immaterial realms in real time. You don't need VR goggles and data gloves to be in ScreenSpace.

P36 / Tuesday, June 17, 2003 10:09 AM
Massive blows (bombs, fires, floods, earthquakes and gradual destruction by plague or by pollution) are inherent to the life processes of a city. It is in these disaster areas, where the buildings have collapsed, their inhabitants dead or evacuated, that the meaning that once organized urban space evaporates. Sign and symbol are reduced to sheer materiality.

The other edge of the WTC tragedy is that NYC has been given the chance to radically re-invent itself. It seems that memorial plays a larger role in reconstruction every day. Is this crippling or necessary? Certainly we must remember, but is it possible that too consuming a memorial will be a scar that the city not only will never forget, but can never recover from? What is the relationship between event, memory, memorial, and recovery?

takes for granted the obscenity of fame and the star architectural system.

I do not see these individuals or young pulp groups attending world conferences on architecture and swapping stories with Charles Correa or Daniel Libeskind. Nor do I see them appearing at biennales, although they may be tempted soon enough. When someone like Peter Eisenman says "we'll be seeing you again," I don't think these pulp architects would be rude, but I fancy they would not be seeing him again. They may not even turn up at these events at all. In this way our imagined new movement-in-progress is an underclass including those whose thinking might not conventionally impact on architecture.

There is nothing visually or identifiably similar in the pulp practices that appear to be working at the edge of architecture. As yet they have not branded their work so that we can recognize their future projects or identify a common practice. In this case they are not and may never be a community at all outside these papers. They move, their work is in progress; their solutions often partial, their destinations restless. From Delhi to Tokyo, from Graz to Texas, from Terezin to Toronto, from Arlington to Yale, they are working in the seams of other disciplines.

Such a new movement would under usual circumstances come to a stop. The usual circumstances involve the critic, the world and the text. The critic organizes a critical enquiry suiting the strategies. The written project becomes a tactical way of expressing larger strategies, greater agendas. There are many examples of this in the 20th century. We are familiar with this way of scripting architectural practices and work into critical groupings like Post-Modernism, Late Modernism, Neo-Modernism and more recently Liquid Architecture and Neo-Expressionism. Charles Jencks is one of the more well known critics. He demonstrated a brilliant, fluid talent at addressing change before it received critical recognition. From Post-Modernism to the new paradigm, chaos, and Morphogenetic Architecture, often his own critical recognition stood in for the professional triumph.

No mean feat!

But it is the inherent ambiguity implied in the phrase "a movement in progress" which naturally resists this kind of grouping. Many are architects who have left but haven't arrived yet. Some are practitioners in other disciplines displaying a new approach and thinking that will re-shape our environments. Many desire to stay away from more conventional terminology: the city, the town, the streetscape, the road.

Even the word "architecture" proves too narrow for this vision-to-come.

The Pulp challenge

The Pulp challenge then is both to architecture as a discipline and as a profession. To many of these Pulp practices, architecture as a profession is already defunct. Much contemporary profiled architecture is propelled by the self-arranging processes of fame and the media. Meanwhile there is a gentleness in some new architecture that rejects such developments. This gentleness does not preclude rigor, is not as velvet as it appears, and rebellion dusts more than the radical surface.

How, they ask, faced with urban decline, deadspaces and unsafe environments, can architecture make a difference? And how might it do this without the hubris in the profession creeping in once more? And without spectacular but

---

MCT / Tue, 17 Jun 2003 20:51:11 -0400

For purposes of discussion, let me distinguish two closely related issues your questions raise: disaster and memorial. No thinker has subjected the notion or, more precisely, the non-notion of disaster to more rigorous reflection than Maurice Blanchot. In The Writing of the Disaster, he maintains: "There is no reaching the disaster. Out of reach is he whom it threatens, whether from afar or close up, it is impossible to say: the infiniteness of the threat has in some way broken every limit. We are on the edge of the disaster without being able to situate it in the future: it is rather always already past, and yet we are on the edge or under the threat, all these formulations which would imply the future – that which is yet to come – if the disaster were not that which does not come, that which has put a stop to every arrival."

The disaster "does not come… has put a stop to every arrival." Bombs, fires, floods, earthquakes are not disasters senso strictissmo but are traces of a disaster that occurs by not

occurring. The non-event of the disaster is never present as such; rather, the disaster disrupts (as if from within) the presence of whatever is. To identify specific events with the disaster as such is to miss what is most disturbing about all disruption. What makes "disastrous" events so terrifying is the way they trace what can never be represented or apprehended.

The disaster bears a complex relation to meaning. On the one hand, the disaster hollows out every meaning that seems solid and secure. The point here is not merely that the literal destruction you note calls into question meaning. Rather, the trace of the disaster – and we can never apprehend more than the trace – exposes the fragility of all meaning. On the other hand, whatever meaning affirm emerges from the disaster. Meaning is inevitably baseless; there is no firm foundation upon which meaning rests. This is not to imply, however, that there is no meaning; there are meanings and these meanings are constantly forming, deforming and reforming in the absence of any security or certainty. The question of memorial as well a

memory is no less tangled. Again, I cite Blanchot: "The disa is related to forgetfulness – forgetfulness without memor motionless retreat of what has not been treated – the imme perhaps. To remember forgetfully." It would take many page develop this insight. Obviously, the WTC tragedy has raised issues of memorial and memory in a very poignant way. Bu thinking about these problems has been limited by a litera which is shortsighted. While the concern to create a fitting memorial to this specific event is understandable, it is nec to take a broad historical perspective. In the larger schem things, this tragedy is but one among many. In the not-too-c future, this event will look very different than it does today. must also be honest about the political manipulation of thi event and the efforts to memorialize it. I believe the preocc tion with a literal memorial is a serious mistake. If one por Blanchot's point, an alternative way to think memorial emer The disaster, I have suggested, is the non-occurrence in ar through which every event occurs.

irrelevant contemporary neo-modern buildings, how can architecture make a difference?

There is nothing naive or ridiculous in these questions. And – almost a hundred years later – it is timely to ask that question again, architecture or revolution? Perhaps it is a naivety that rejects spectacle and representation without yet knowing what this rejection leads to. This includes the new experiments in mixed reality, ubiquitous programming and trans-programming, A-life, nano-technology and various other soon-to-be-named processes. It is possible that these experiments will no longer be confined to the narrow utopia of digital art and virtual reality.

Then there are those outside the discipline and there are many – graphic, fashion, web designers, systems architects, computer scientists, engineers, bio-geneticists, mathematicians, skateboarders, interactive artists – who are sitting and working at the edge of architecture. These various individuals and collaborations work without always knowing that they possess the talent and ideas that could re-shape our cities and our lives.

Sampling, transformation and simulation are all options incorporated within pulp architecture. Put these along with topologies, surfaces, weaves, patterns and folds and we begin to see the new adventure. Or do we miss the point, avoid the mediocre and elevate these strategies beyond their usefulness?

Would this make Pulp merely a freshly repetitive intelligence like those pulp novels re-framing the sensation of the underworld? Or could this be a long overdue, sophisticated refusal to negotiate architecture as we see it? Could it represent what many of these new practices think: dazzling metaphors and alibis for a future architecture stealthily leaving architects behind? "Hiphop" and "house" may appear unassertive in its looting of a musical past, as horizontal as it might be un-intensive, but a rave flattens out of course, identifies its own subversive power and moves on. It must. Intense as it might tempt the reckless, pulp architecture may prove to need the edge of irresponsibility to appear so talented.

The final frontier

Pulp is arbitrary, random and a fruit machine, a flash of orange in Tarantino, the manga frame broken by Japanese pain, reflection, excess, redemption, a passage from Ezekial, a tarantula on an angel cake, an idoru, a yahoo lounge in Narita airport, a character called *hiro* protagonist or low-rez. Pulp is a *samurai* sword talking back to its future user, a French girl softly asking whose chopper is that? Like everything, pulp is only the street, lying in wait, just as Duchamp said, waiting to take over from the deadmuseums, the deadmalls, dead architecture.

If movement itself is essential to our contemporary existence then Pulp Architecture can only ever be a movement-in-progress. Pulp is theory and anti-theory. Pulp is an architecture that seems to wish to stay on the edge. It may be an architecture that respects but rejects the star architecture system of individualized spectacles.

No total architectures!

Pulp challenges existing architecture as much as it challenges architecture already on the edge. In a contemporary condition "between" rather than "within," Pulp is an architecture informed and fashioned from and programmed by, film, street culture, art, play, terror, surveillance, the hacker ethic and new media....

---

ce the disaster never takes place, it cannot be repre- It is, therefore, outside of memory or, in Blanchot's terms, orial. This immemorial is not eternal but, to the contrary, found temporality, which is never present. The disaster is t that was never present, which eternally returns as the hat never arrives to disrupt the present that never is. To - or perhaps disfigure – this disaster is to trace the within which death and, more important, life arise and ay.

ate unknown
s that within your characterization of disaster as an orial event, there lies a supposition about the effect of r, and the close personal relationship we necessarily have . The traces of disaster, which "trace the horizon within eath and… life arise and pass away," become a fear that nds any specific event to become part of everyday usness. Is the ghost of this fear, recoverable only in an

extremely personal way, the only possible "memorial," continuously affecting our actions and our relationships to the world?

MCT / Tue, 22 Jul 2003 15:27:35 -0400
You raise two distinct but related questions: the personal, or more, precisely the impersonal; and fear, or, more precisely, dread.

The disaster is not personal but is the approach of the impersonal, which can never be properly named. It is precisely this impersonality that incites dread. As Kierkegaard taught us, dread is the response to the awareness of no-thing. Fear, by contrast, is always brought about by something specific. But dread has no object and, therefore, is much more disconcerting. Because the disaster never becomes determinate, it is, in a sense, nothing. This nothingness unsettles us in the most profound way. To insist that the impersonality of the disaster brings dread which is the relation to nothing is not to suggest that it is unrelated to us in our individuality. The contrary, as Heidegger teaches us, dread singles us out in our individual

subjectivity. Paradoxically, only by facing the disaster do I become an individual.

P36 / Date unknown
In this realm of questioning are conventional literalizations of the memorial (which recall only death or destruction, but never the questions of being, the fear of death and destruction) relevant in the long term in any way? How can one pass this feeling on to future generations? Is it at all possible? Or even necessary?

MCT / Date unknown
Most memorials are banal. They are intended to memorialize a particular individual or event. As such, the memorial is supposed to render permanent what is transitory. Such efforts are, of course, futile because the transitory cannot be fixed. Memorials intended to remember become monuments to forgetting. Visit any cemetery or monument – even when the names remain they are

Of course the list can never be closed!

It is important to remember: Pulp architecture is not an approach to architecture that believes that it can rescue a type of architecture that might otherwise have gone missing. Pulp architecture is an attitude that may ultimately have nothing to do with architecture at all!

Or Pulp may be a naive attempt to resist the architecture that already appears to be scripted by forces beyond. We toggle architectural parti, we google the future, we scroll through other lives as we scratch out other buildings and scrawl our own future.

Pulp may resist an architecture we have no right to resist!

So tell me if you will

Where did Pulp come from?

Is it chance invention, a ground swell or a critical calculation?

It was no coincidence that I had just returned from travels in Japan, from visiting Tokyo, Nagoya, Kyoto and Osaka. It was also no coincidence that as I stood in the middle of the Roppongi crossing in Tokyo the word "pulp" seemed to jump out at me.

On looking back it is possible I should have rightly called this Punk Architecture. There are obvious similarities between the relentless branding and celebrity cults in architectural spectacle and the situation at the end of the 1970s. The recent death of Joe Strummer, the lead singer of the Clash gives us an opportunity to consider whether this may have resonance to that time past, and lead to a growing street activity of gentle or less gentle outrage.

Are the parallels ridiculous? Strummer, real name John Graham Mellor, was a punk rocker born in Ankara, Turkey. He went to public school in England, founded in the late '70s one of the most important bands of the 1980s, during an era when extravagance began creeping back into society. Who can forget "The Guns of Brixton" or "Lost in the Supermarket"?

It was impossible to miss the coincidence of the death of Joe Strummer at the same time as the release of the 6 architectural visions for the new World Trade Project in Manhattan. Was I alone in thinking this a rather predictable spectacle for an architecture, an action, an event which we wish not to be so predictable?

Surely not!

Pulp architecture does not exist yet, but in a way it does. For if it is work in transit, then those transitional stages exist at all times. Pulp architecture is not the work that becomes the museum of the future. Pulp architecture would not offer a vision for New York that must last for eternity. Nor is it work that makes these visions possible. Pulp architecture is a rehearsal. It is that stage before accepting what architecture knows it can become. Youthful in its excitement, much of it might be in the hands and consoles of the young, but it is hardly immature.

Pulp architecture is more at home with the Citroën car as the exact equivalent of the great Gothic cathedrals as Roland Barthes claimed in the 1950s. Pulp architecture is the final frontier, the anti-thesis of slick. It reviews the production values connected to architecture. It may need luxury to create it but will always lie beyond luxury. From the street up, it is an architecture generated by game strategies. Ultimately like Pulp itself it is a manipulation of code. It is an intervention in a system that has no predetermined form.

---

anonymous — they are the names of the nameless ones. Letters etched in stone invariable read: You will be forgotten. By memorializing forgetting, memorials succeed in their failure.

P36 / Friday, August 01, 2003 11:12 AM
(Jen) I spent time in Croatia a few weeks ago and was struck at a certain moment by this scene: My Croatian friend, Satchi, speaking heatedly of America's incendiary role in the world (the evil empire) — with Kenny from "South Park" plastered across his chest and Eminem remixed blasting over the car stereo of his Ford Focus.

Clearly in recent years for a multitude of reasons there has been an increasingly obvious juxtaposition (or overlay) of anti-American sensibilities with cultural colonialism. It seems that the binary opposition that dissolved with the end of the cold war is beginning to re-assert itself within the idea of America itself. Is this conflict sustainable? If not, how will it resolve itself?

MCT / Saturday, 02 Aug 2003 07:45:06 -0400
This is a difficult and an important question. The conflict you note is symptomatic of the deep ambivalence many people and countries feel about the United States. In many ways, American popular culture is one of the most powerful political forces in the world today. But the issue is quite complicated. As recent debates about the FCC's effort to take the deregulation of media to another level have shown, the power of media — in the broadest sense of the term — is increasingly concentrated in a few multi-national companies. It is important to note that not all of these are owned by America. Consider, for example, Rupert Murdoch as well as Bertlesman. Much of the content on the various networks these organizations owned is produced by and reflective of the U.S. There is simply no other place in the world capable of producing this kind of material on this scale. This is not to say, of course, that other countries don't have their film, publishing, etc. industries. Art and culture — high as well as low — have long been used by many countries to extend national power. But with

current technology, the scope and scale of this change. As world becomes more wired, different cultures will increas come into contact with each other. While one might hope t eventually influence will run in both directions, in the inter mediate run, America will exercise considerably more pow other countries. The question is: Given the choice between and-roll and the mosque and veil, what will most young pe choose? I think it is important to note that the use of media popular culture to disseminate ideas is not always negativ Indeed, I believe it is possible to deploy these technologie other ends. That is why I have founded the Global Educatic Network. But the challenges are considerable and it is too to tell if we can be successful.

Can the tension be sustained? Two responses: First, I d foresee any end to the continuing spread of and fascinatio American popular culture. Second, I cannot believe that the perspective informing the current administration in Washi is sustainable. We are in a very strange time warp, which, i

ast twenty years, the urban youth
taking grey concrete walls to task.
nd, which arose at the end of the 70s,
the world over as graffiti. Among
ving number of participators, there
e artists who conduct intellectual
ations with each other wholly within
culture's unwritten laws and stan-
this academic dialogue the wall sur-
as an interface. Today we have to
e that as a consequence of this pro-
ntellectual battle an exceedingly
and highly developed formal idiom
erged, one that deserves a place in
ional architecture.

Maurer United Architects,
Graffiti Construction, 2001 (from
Japanese magazine *IDEA*,
January 2001)

Turner Brooks, Rome Fellowship,
American Academy in Rome

Klein Dytham Architects, Tokyo,
Japan

---

ays, is a continuation of the culture wars of the 1960s. As
come all too clear, the ability of the Bush administration to
agenda to the American people is in no small part a
n of manipulation of the media. The right has always been
nore media savvy than the left in this country. But I am
of a Hegelian to believe that history moves by a process
ectical reversal. If today's network society teaches us
g, it is that the age of Empire is over. It is simply astonish-
hear all the talk of empire circulating today. Again, we
e honest; America has unsurpassed military and economic
And we must acknowledge that most of Europe has, in
outsourced military operations to the U.S. This decision
d positive and negative consequences. On the positive
has allowed much of Europe to develop very sophisticated
welfare systems. On the negative side, it has resulted in a
power on the world scene. I think that the course America
following will necessarily end in failure and reverse
Not only will the U.S. meet continuing resistance from

forces that are impossible to contain but the economic demands
of guns and butter are not sustainable. As the economic cost of
the Bush agenda becomes increasingly clear, resistance to it will
grow. The frustrating thing at the moment is that the Democrats
are offering no constructive and persuasive alternative.

P36 / Friday, August 08, 2003 10:25 AM

As the Berlin wall fell, it atomized and reappeared all over the
world, everywhere from Palestine to the privileged gated
community. In an effort to simplify an increasingly complex
world, we build walls that keep out the other. There is a natural
social resistance to overlap; people do not like other kinds of
people.

As an architectural element the wall has enormous
meaning, in contrast to the proliferation of digital transference.
Connection versus separation. Can these two drives exist
simultaneously in constant interplay, or will one win over the
other. If separation wins, the possibility exists for a world

connected digitally, but with no physical interaction among
different cultures.

MCT / Monday, August 11, 2003 9:45 AM

As you suggest, the Berlin Wall was "atomized and reappeared all
over the world" – in both a literal and figurative sense. I have a
fragment of the wall in my study as a constant reminder of
everything that structure continues to mean. The problem of
"connection vs. separation" is, of course, as old as life itself. All
living beings must cultivate both individuality and commonality.
From my point of view, connection and separation are dialecti-
cally related – each presupposes the other and, therefore,
neither can be what it is apart from the other. Throughout history,
different technologies have created different possibilities for
connection and separation. What distinguishes current digital
and network technologies is the range and speed of connection.
I do not think the issue is as simple as people not liking each
other. Contact with difference always raises difficult questions

Intimacy

I have seen Frank fight with Peter, and Peter fight with Bernard. I have seen Daniel whisper to Frank and Peter fight with Daniel. I have heard Herb rag Daniel and Peter rag Herb. I have seen Peter fight with Michael and Philip fight with them all. And then make up. I have seen Bernard deny jet-lag and Rem go off with Jacques to the Noucamp in Barcelona. I have seen John remain detached and Philip come back again. I have watched people come and go in the lobby of the Hotel Architecture and you think you recognize exactly what I am talking about.

For some reason in the profession of architecture there is a tendency to scorn the ideas and projects of other architects. Taking sides, making waves, occupying positions and destroying others, these gladiators of ideology look for the weakest link. Some think of this a natural dynamic. A creative way to make sure we get the architecture we have already thought about, but not in our own minds. The democracy in this includes rancor, bitterness, envy and personal disaster. Suicide even! It is a kind of natural hardball, as if you should disappear if you cannot play this.

If you cannot stand the heat, Peter will say, or Philip or Daniel, then get out of the kitchen!

Peter, Michael, Daniel, Bernard, Frank... whatever, whoever!

Can anyone really remain detached from the architecture the world has made for itself? Is there in this hopeless task the potential of an architecture gone missing? And if so what could that architecture be?

The Professor of Night had been preparing his ideas for the Faculty meeting. He was working on the idea of a parallel architecture. He couldn't find a name for this, at least a name that would stick. He wouldn't dream of calling it architecture of nothing but he did sympathize with those who thought it was a work-in-progress that never actually progresses. But those architectures forever shifting, informed by the ever-present fear and security didn't entirely convince him.

What was an architecture unable to respond to HIV aids? What was an architecture unable to respond to the grief of the twin towers in New York? How architecture mourned the hypnotic, but could not deflect the bullet's trajectory, nor heal the gun-shot wound of the civilian or the stabbing in the department store.

The Professor of Night picked the short straw.

This was a new intimacy, a way of avoiding that degree zero again. Prepare yourselves. Look for the spaces in between. Go for the blind spots in architecture. Look for the pockets. Give back to surroundings all that has been lost, and all that will remain being lost. Alter the programs as only you can. Re-write the software and re-occupy architecture from the street up. Show others the architecture that they do not know exists, not the architecture scripted before them.

And grafted onto all those buildings that remain in New York might be nothing but the degree zero of architecture. And not only when the sun sets and the light diagonizes in on September 11th each year!

The zero is the fullest space from which to start over, the Professor of Night wrote on his Powerbook.

A single sentence.

The first sentence of the book he would write. Everything would flow from these words. Nothing else would be possible. Everything else would be possible.

and poses challenging dilemmas. Unless one is naive or ideologically blinded, the encounter with alternative visions of reality makes it necessary to rethink one's own perspective. Such reflection can be both liberating and troubling. Thus, there is both attraction to and dread of increasing interconnection. When dread dominates, there is a tendency to seek security by reinforcing old walls and building new ones. Unfortunately, we are seeing this throughout the world today — and nowhere more so than in the U.S. This is part of what is at stake in much neo-fundamentalist religion and neo-conservative politics.

I think the two rhythms of connection and separation not only can but must exist simultaneously. If either overwhelms the other, it negates itself. A balance between competing tendencies is never accomplished and the only relevant question concerns the degree of tension sustained at any given time. The proliferation of digital technologies increases connectedness and this, in turn, creates anxieties and uncertainties that lead to an effort to secure separation and isolation, which is, in the final analysis, increasingly difficult if not impossible. There will always be physical interaction among different cultures because life depends on it if for no other reason — and there clearly are other reasons — than the fact that the earth's ecosystem cannot be sustained without interactions. As we are learning every day, such interactions breed conflict as much or perhaps more than understanding. If there is to be any possibility of hope, however, it must come from greater understanding through increasing interrelation.

CARACAS CASE STUDY:
THE CULTURE OF THE INFORMAL CITY

MARJETICA POTRC

Developments in the Caracas metropolis depend profoundly on informal influences. The effects are so strong, particularly in times of economic crises, that even parts of the formal city get caught in their wake. In the past, Barrios have not been registered on city maps, nor has anybody taken serious interest in their form, improvised production methods, or culture.

To break the taboo of the emerging informal city is, for many in public administration, impossible after ignoring the situation for so long. To confront the growing and present Barrio is to recognize its contribution as the principal expression of our civilization.

The Barrios are by no means perfect environments, but in their totality they present a Superstructure with a high degree of self-organization. The processes and patterns of creative dynamics inside the Barrios could deliver tangible suggestions which could profoundly change the vision of future legislation, affecting planning strategies for Caracas and other Latin American cities.

The project attempts to find answers to the paradigms of growth and organization in the Barrios: how informal cities grow by destroying their traditional organization-systems, and how they organize themselves in an apparent chaos by means of informal interventions. The auto-organization and production without jurisdiction has resulted in an impressive democratic building that presents a better answer to urban problems than the official strategies of the city administration. Traditional academic knowledge is put aside to enter the Barrio, a place of practical built solutions to urban challenges – executed results that should no longer be ignored.

Caracas Case Study
2003
18 drawings
22.5 x 30.0 cm
Courtesy the artist,
Max Protetch Gallery and
Caracas Case Project

NORTH AMERICANS LIKE TO THINK OF THEIR HOMES IN GREEN ARCADIA: IT IS OPEN AND SHARED WITH OTHERS

SOUTH AMERICANS LIKE TO ENCIRCLE THEIR TERRITORY FIRST

1

THE WALLED CITIES OF CARACAS

BARRED WINDOWS

BARRIO: HAVING ONLY A FEW ENTRIES TO A BARRIO HELPS CONTROL THE TERRITORY

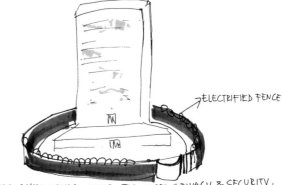

ELECTRIFIED FENCE

GATED COMMUNITIES OFFER THE MOST PRIVACY & SECURITY. THEY MAKE SURE THAT PRIVATE AND PUBLIC SPHERES ARE CLEARLY DIVIDED.

2

THE HILLS OF CARACAS

FEEL BEAUTIFUL AND THREATENING AT THE SAME TIME

BARRIOS EXPAND INTO THE CREEKS
THAT FLOW INTO THE CITY
FROM MOUNT AVILA

NATURE : MOUNT AVILA, BARRIOS AND HIGHRISES,
THEY ARE ALL GROWING

BARRIOS GROW HIGHER THAN HIGHRISES

3

THE CITY IN A HOUSE

THE VITALITY OF CARACAS CAN BE SEEN IN A HOUSE

ALL HOUSES
IN THE BARRIOS GROW

AND LIVE FROM WITHIN

A HOUSE IS NEVER ABOUT A PLAN,
A HOUSE IS A BODY

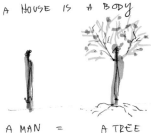

A MAN   =   A TREE   = A COLUMN FOR
                                         A HOUSE

4

GROWING AND CLAIMING THE TERRITORY

IN RURAL ALABAMA, HOUSES GROW HORIZONTALLY

WORKSHOP   RESIDENCE   ORIGINAL CORE UNIT

EATING PLACE &
SHOP

54

IN HONG KONG, HOMES GROW ON THE OUTSIDE
OF RESIDENTIAL HIGHRISES

IN DOWTOWN BELGRADE, HOUSES GROW ON TOP OF
BUILDINGS

RECENTLY, RESIDENTS OF THESE TWO HOMES
BUILT A WALL SO PEOPLE COULD NOT LOOK
AT THEM, AND VICE VERSA—

→ RED PITCHED ROOF

→ A WALL

RECALLS THE ARCHITECTURE OF
WEST BANK JEWISH SETTLEMENTS
PERCHED ON TOP OF HILLS

FORTRESS-LIKE
ARCHITECTURE

IT'S BEAUTIFUL, BUT ALSO FEELS MEDIEVAL,
SIMILAR TO THE VIEW I ADMIRE WHILE
DRIVING THROUGH TUSCANY

WHICH BRINGS ME TO THE GROWING HOUSE,
A CASE STUDY OF ALICIA'S HOME, LOCATED ON
THE TOP OF LA VEGA, A BARRIO OF 200.000 PEOPLE

MOST IMPORTANT IS THE STRATEGIC POSITION:
ALICIA IS ABLE TO SURVEY THE GROUND BELOW

7

8

ALICIA SAID THAT SHE IS HAPPY HER HOUSE
IS SITUATED AT THE CORNER OF THE SETTLEMENT
BECAUSE SHE COULD ADD ONTO IT.

THE ONLY PROBLEM SEEMED TO BE THAT THERE WAS
AN ELECTRICITY POLE LOCATED RIGHT IN THE MIDDLE
OF THE HOUSE.

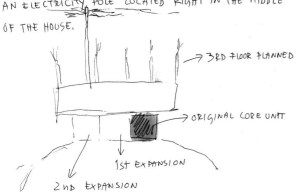

→ 3RD FLOOR PLANNED

→ ORIGINAL CORE UNIT

↓ 1ST EXPANSION

↙ 2ND EXPANSION

→ ORIGINAL CORE UNIT

→ EXPANSION
OF HOUSE
&
APPROPRIATION
OF TERRITORY

WHEN SHE WAS EXPANDING THE HOUSE,
SHE JUST BUILT AROUND THE POLE, AND NOW
BECAUSE OF IT SHE CANNOT BUILD A THIRD FLOOR.

BUILDING HER HOUSE = BUILDING HER LIFE

9

10

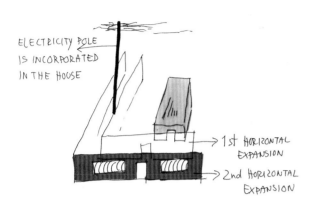

ELECTRICITY POLE
IS INCORPORATED
IN THE HOUSE

→ 1st HORIZONTAL
EXPANSION

→ 2nd HORIZONTAL
EXPANSION

11

PLANNED EXPANSION
THIRD FLOOR

GROWING

12

THE DIVIDED CITY BREEDS INVASIONS

HALF OF CARACAS' POPULATION LIVES IN BARRIOS,
THE OTHER HALF IN THE FORMAL CITY.
THE VERY EXISTENCE OF THE POPULATION AND
ARCHITECTURE IN BOTH HALVES IS THREATENED
BY VARIOUS INVASIONS.

CARACAS INVASION No 1:
BARRIOS ———→ FORMAL CITY

HOT OIL
IS POURED
ON INVADERS

ATTACK OF THE BARRIO INVADERS

13

CARACAS INVASION No 2:
RURAL ———→ URBAN

URBAN
AGRICULTURE

LETTUCE AND RED PEPPERS ARE PLANTED
IN A PUBLIC PARK IN THE CITY CENTER.

WORKSHOPS ARE ORGANIZED TO TEACH RESIDENTS
TO USE HYDROPONIC TECHNOLOGY TO GROW
SMALL SCALE VEGETABLE GARDENS.

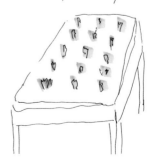

14

56

CARACAS INVASION No 3 = INVASIONS OF THE LAND

LAND EROSION

THE BARRIOS ARE OFTEN IN PHYSICAL DANGER
FROM LAND INVADERS, SETTLERS WHO BUILD
NEW STRUCTURES UP THE SLOPE AND DESTABILIZE
ALREADY EXISTING STRUCTURES.

↓ HOUSES TUMBLE DOWN

↑ WATER RISES

CONSTANT EXPANSION AND CONSTANT EROSION

15

URBAN NEGOTIATION IS CRUCIAL IN CARACAS,
A CITY IN CONSTANT CRISIS AND WITHOUT MUCH HISTORY,
WHERE THE SOCIAL STATE HAS NEVER REALLY
MATERIALIZED.

IT SOUNDS LIKE A PERFECT CASE STUDY FOR
TODAY'S METROPOLIS,
INSTABILITY MAKES YOU RELEVANT.

16

THE WEST BANK = NEGOTIATED TERRITORY

ZONES A, B, C

CONTROLLED BY
A - ISRAELIS WITH SOME
    PALESTINIAN PARTICIPATION
B - HALF-HALF
C - PALESTINIANS WITH
    SOME ISRAELI
    PARTICIPATION

ZONES CHANGE SHAPE ALL THE TIME

SPACE IS IN CONSTANT FLUX IN THE WEST BANK,
SIMILAR TO WHAT ONE FEELS IN THE FAST
GROWING CITIES OF LATIN AMERICA.

17

DIVISIONS BREED NEW FRAMES OF MIND

IN THE WEST BANK, YOU HAVE TWO ROAD SYSTEMS
THAT RARELY INTERSECT
- ONE CONNECTING JEWISH SETTLEMENTS
- THE OTHER ONE CONNECTING PALESTINIAN
  TOWNS AND VILLAGES

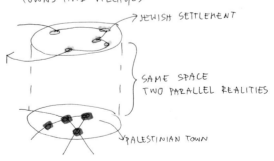

→ JEWISH SETTLEMENT

SAME SPACE
TWO PARALLEL REALITIES

→ PALESTINIAN TOWN

CARACAS' WALLS AND BORDERS ARE WITHIN US.

18

1

5

2

6

4

КАСПАРОВ   КАРПОВ

3

11

9

7

13

14

10

1 Deep Blue vs. Garry Kasparov. May 3, 1997
2 Boris Spassky vs. Bobby Fischer. Reykjavik, September 3, 1972
3 Garry Kasparov vs. Anatoly Karpov, 1985
4 Garry Kasparov vs. Deep Fritz. New York, November 2003

5 *From Russia With Love*, directed by Terence Young, 1964
6 *Seventh Seal*, directed by Ingmar Bergman, 1958
7 *Futureworld*, directed by Richard Heffron, 1976
8 Sonny and Cher, c. 1967
9 Go game

10 *What's New Pussycat*, directed by Clive Donner, 1965
11 Marcel Duchamp and Man Ray
12 Marcel Duchamp and John Cage, 1968
13 HAL eye, from *2001: A Space Odyssey*
14 *Goban*

WET VS. DRY: THE CHESS/GO PROJECT

NEIL DENARI

The Chess/Go project
La Beauté en Avignon, 2000
Unbuilt; reworked in 2003

Architect
Neil M. Denari Architects, Los Angeles

Project team
1999 Neil Denari, Christian Smoeltz
2003 Neil Denari, Matt Trimble

All design work in the publication from 2003

Local architect
Boris Koifman

Client
Jean de Loisy, Chief Curator, *La Beauté en Avignon*

Research and concept development
Caroline Naphegy, Paris

Europe's largest millennium exhibition in 2000, *La Beauté en Avignon*, was a sprawling festival of work whose theme was that of beauty in the contemporary world. Artists such as Gerhard Richter, Björk, Anish Kapoor, Alexander McQueen, and Jean-Luc Godard were asked to create personal worlds of beauty located in sites around the city of Avignon, most notably in the Palais du Pape.

Neil M. Denari Architects was one of four architectural offices invited to participate, and in an abandoned factory building located a few hundred meters outside the medieval walls of the city, we were asked to design an entrance structure based on the aesthetics and strategies of the games of chess and go. This structure would lead to spaces where films depicting chess and go scenes would be projected.

Auto-human

For almost two centuries, chess has been a measure, a kind of litmus test, of both human and machine intelligence. As early as 1833, when Charles Babbage conceived his Analytical Engine, he thought if it could be built, that it would be able to play chess. And again in 1949, Claude Shannon, the great information theorist, analyzed chess as a diagram of the complexity of life. Clearly, the issue of thinking machines, from automatons, to HAL in Kubrick's *2001*, to Kasparov's matches with Deep(er) Blue in 1996 and 1997 and Fritz in 2002, has sponsored a new arrangement of knowledge between technology, media, and human thought.

Inverted parallel logics

Go is the most ancient and perhaps most inscrutable of strategic games. While it has been played for thousands of years in Asia, has not been used to determine levels of intelligence in the West. Nevertheless, its own sense of logic as strategy and as aesthetic can be easily compared to chess. Indeed, there is a kind of "diagonal symmetry" between the two games, as if one image were to be mirrored, then inverted in Photoshop for instance.

Wet vs. dry

Both are played on gridded boards, each an indication of a neutralized, original ground, yet chess is vertical, arborescent, and hierarchical while go is horizontal, rhizomatic, and non-hierarchical. The two games, in fact, summarize the formal conditions of many phenomena in the world, including cities, where monuments and clearly defined programs (*dry* or point to point) have given way to vague and exceedingly repetitious fields (*wet* or fluid).

As part of a larger assembly of projects and installations that comprise *La Beauté* exhibition in Avignon, France, the Chess/Go project was a response to these comparative conditions between the two games. Through the research of strategies of movement, logic systems, and Artificial Intelligence, in both its cinematic and technological representation, as well as the emotions of madness, passion, and confrontation, the project is an attempt at spatializing the aesthetics and logic of chess and go.

Chess   Go

Mirror/invert

Wet/go

Dry/chess

Thinking

Compare/contrast

Chess	Go
Western	Eastern
Hierarchical	Non-hierarchical
Arborescent	Rhizomatic
Militaristic	Passive
Kill/take opponent	Surround opponent
Vertical	Horizontal
Strategic	Intuitive
B&W grid board	Neutral board, B&W stones

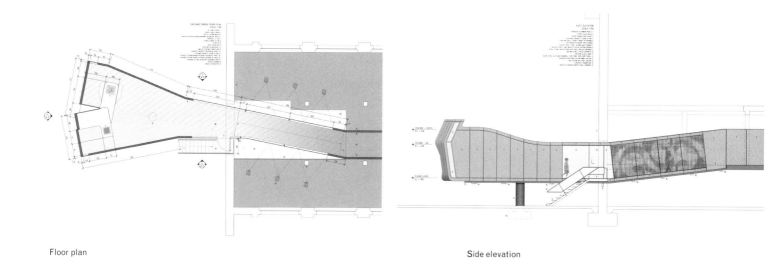

Floor plan   Side elevation

Interior

Electronic boards

Zvi Hecker, Rafi Segal and Eyal Weizman: Correspondence

From Perspecta 36 to Zvi Hecker, Rafi Segal and Eyal Weizm
Title: Perspecta 36, the Yale architectural journal
Your work deals both directly and indirectly with the folly ar
contradiction of contemporary imperialism.

In Iraq today there is a strong resistance, not necessari
the removal of Saddam Hussein (a single violent event), but
the occupation and by extension to the re-construction of Ir
In this sense resistance against the occupying power becon
resistance against architecture. How can a country be rebui
when there is a residual resistance to the creation of space
architecture) after space has been willfully destroyed?

From Eyal Weizman to Rafi Segal and Perspecta 36
Title: Re: FW: 36 Perspecta
I understand this question to refer to what may or should ha
to the architecture of power when power is suddenly un-plug

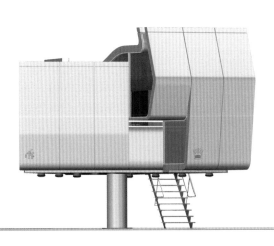

Front elevation

Exterior view from plaza

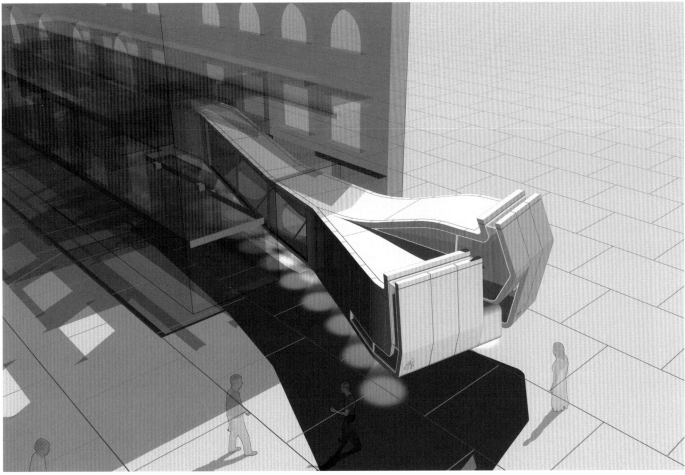

Aerial view

cally, when empires and occupations are dismantled, their cture remains largely in place and gets appropriated by ly formed post-colonial regime. Paradoxically, this s of accommodation may reproduce or mimic some of the social, political or military patterns. In that respect at -inhabiting architecture and mimicking the habit that is ded within its spatial syntax appears to recreate similar elationships in space.

en the spatial-political infrastructure of colonialism is ct the colonial villas get inhabited by a new financial e palaces by a political one, the prisons filled with new rsive" enemies, and the government buildings of the ers prop up a new regime. Moreover, the dispersed x of military bases happens to suit (as if by chance) a new phy of resistance. Often the very same regions and cities sisted colonialism now resist the post- (or neo-) colonial

example: the matrix of British police and military bases

known as Tagart-forts that were built throughout Palestine in an effort to repress the Arab revolt of the 1930s were "perfectly" located to serve the Israeli state that replaced it in 1948, and were later used to contain and supervise the Arab-Palestinian population that remained within an otherwise cleansed Palestine.

One of the many mistakes of the U.S. as it occupied Iraq (going there in the first place was the main one) was to reuse the very same symbols of power that were built and evacuated by the Baathist regime of Saddam. The obvious examples are the Abu-Ghraib prison (then and now a political prison), and the Green Zone, an extra-territorial American island (where American soldiers mobile phones operate on a local American dialing code) that was once a Saddam inner city Palace-enclave. These are just two well-known examples of a practice that has turned routine.

On the other hand, and this is where an alternative model may be relevant, when regimes are replaced there may be a short period of uncertainty before ideology accommodates the

existing spatial infrastructure. When architecture and power no longer overlap there is a fleeting a moment of opportunity. Suddenly, the once feared and awesome structures may become nothing but piles of bricks whose horrific associations promise to fade away in time. Think of the many piles of stone (otherwise referred to as archaeology) that were once sites of intolerable violence, battles, incarceration, executions, etc...

Last week in a meeting I attended with a group of architects that included the Palestinian deputy minister of planning in Ramallah, we discussed the fate of the settlements/colonies in Gaza that Israel may evacuate. If the homes were to be left standing, Palestinian planners were warning, the Palestinian elite – so called Sulta – may use these as "luxury" suburbs, fort themselves up, replicating and reproducing the similar spatio-social violence and patronization of the Israeli occupation.

The inclination of all of us was to want to see the demolition of this civilian occupation of petite bourgeois red roofed homes and gardens that embodies so much aggression (both explicit

MODERN IN THE MIDDLE

SANDY ISENSTADT

Any modernism that will last must have its roots in what has gone before.[1]
House and Garden, 1933

But whereas the concern of the twenties had been with the modernity of the house, the concern of the mid-thirties – by which time the ideology had become fairly well established and its adherents could relax a bit – was to reconcile the *avant garde* esthetic to images and values traditionally adhering to "house" and "home."[2] William Jordy, 1972

—— 1
Richardson Wright, "Will Our Ancestors Shudder at Modernist Architecture?" *House and Garden* (November 1933), p. 30.

—— 2
"The Domestication of Modern: Marcel Breuer's Ferry Cooperative Dormitory at Vassar College," *The Impact of European Modernism in the Mid-Twentieth Century* (New York: Oxford University Press, 1972), p. 167.

3 ——
"Architecture – Not Style," *Progressive Architecture* (December 1948), pp. 49, 120, 122, 138. Many architectural discussions reflected similar concerns. For example, Davison, "Effect of Style on Cost," *Architectural Record*, no. 65 (April 1929), pp. 402–9, removed the historical connotations from historical styles to arrive at the pure efficiencies of a plan, or Gropius's "Eight Steps Toward a Solid Architecture," published in February 1954 in *Architectural Forum* and incorporated in *The Scope of Total Architecture* (1955): each of the eight steps involves rejecting a former preoccupation with style, addressing "the client's real needs," and gaining technical skills.

Utopian modernism entailed the construction of an entire world of human and machine based upon communal experiment and advanced material production. Social prophecy and technological revelation were fused in its aesthetic vision. As modernism's message broadened in the 1930s beyond its far-seeing progenitors, idealist doctrines relaxed, as Jordy suggested and *House and Garden* insisted, and modernists began to address a wider range of values including many conventional ones, that is, values that were both external and antecedent to modernism. By the 1950s, assimilating the radical edge of architectural modernism to the standard patterns of consumer culture had become something of an avocation. With their founding commitment to advanced means of production, however, adherents of modern architecture continued to claim their work transcended the shortsighted obsessions of the present day. As *Progressive Architecture* said in 1948: "Modern design – design of our time – is not a style. It is a solution to modern problems in modern terms." The concern for "style" or "art" was premature, the editors thought, and should be addressed only after "the social and technical problems have been fully solved. It's time today to get down to real work on those problems, and not sit in our offices worrying about art." Addressing modern problems validated a modern mission in terms that outstripped style.[3] But with traditional styles competitive in cost and with major construction innovations like steel frames, reinforced concrete, and curtain walls more than half a century old by then, a modernist claim of parity with technological advance was simply not convincing, and in postwar America the existing social fabric had come through depression and war healthier than ever. Modernism appeared in the 1950s, to Americans at least, in the context of a proliferation of products in diverse materials, finishes, sizes, and styles of design. With its formal traits easily identifiable, and a comfort-first, mix-n-match mentality predominant, the glass walls and spare, cubic forms of modern architecture seemed more a matter for personal taste than social destiny.

Given this context, modern architecture was increasingly presented in professional and popular journals as being, if not transcendent, then simply the best among competing design options. In many cases, modern was said to combine the best

and latent) and environmental stupidity. But by leaving these structures standing (this is, if Israel does not level these structures altogether) an opportunity exists for a more potent and subtle act of architectural critique. Instead of using these structures of power for the very purpose they were designed to perform (the single family homes as single family homes, the military bases as a military bases), acts of subversion, adaptation and especially the complete break of the prescribed connection between structure, program and use, these left over structures could be reused in a totally different way. The sociologist Abdul Maliq Simone described the way in which local communities in Johannesburg invaded office buildings of the apartheid regime – the very locations where evil was administered – and turned them into chaotic places of informal life and trade.

The jury is still out on what the use of the settlement homes in Gaza could be, but the architecturally prescribed power structure will be handed over to the formless powers of daily need. This phenomenon is roughly what the situationists termed

detournement – a practice of architectural critique that operates through the bizarre matching of new uses to existing structures. This detournement may help turn spatial power on its head – but here the collaboration of Palestinian politics is essential.

Regarding the "resistance against architecture," and the way a country (Iraq?) could be rebuilt, a new order representing Iraqis must consider subverting rather then reusing the existing spatial infrastructure of power. If a democratic Iraqi government uses the spatial infrastructure left by the Saddamists (and now the U.S.) in the same way it was planned and built, it will inevitably replicate the animosity it needs to undo. How liberating it would be to see these bases and prisons become something of what Maliq described as the fate of the apartheid offices…

From Zvi Hecker to Eyal Weizman
Title: About Mankind
Hi Eyal, I am back from Istanbul, where Ottoman architecture reigns superb and its food still tastes great.

A SHORT HISTORY OF MANKIND
In the last 5000 years of human history we have changed little. We are still less then two meters high, we still walk o legs, we reproduce the same way and we eat nearly the sa food. Also our psychological build up changed very little. V believe in gods, we look for leader to lead us, we are scare the unknown and we look for protection and security. Our is that of a caveman.

Though we ourselves changed very little we have char the world around us. We have produced a lot of new toys "t please the time" as Brodsky calls it. The toys brought mixe blessing and a lot of maintenance.

More maintenance will be needed as the planet earth affected by the growing needs of the growing mankind (po tion) shows signs of fatigue. As there is no certainty that something will be done on time, we might return to the cav this time for good.

features of other styles and more generally obviated the issue of choice altogether. It offered the benefits of all with the drawbacks of none and so was able to remain unique by mediating extremes. Between bland boxes and sentimental claptrap, there was modern. Between ever-newer technologies and timeless nature, there was modern. Between the promise of progress and the wealth of the past; between overly-idealistic reforms and head-in-the-sand conservatism; between the public and the private; between the rational and the romantic: modern was in the middle.

A clean reticent frame: a changing landscape drama

> The opposition of nature and machine is a device of interpretation, not a fact of experience.[4] Edgar Kaufmann, Jr.

One polar pair brought together by modern architecture was geometric in character. *Interiors* magazine, for example, reviewed in 1947 "modern rooms of the last fifty years." What editors called "the present synthesis" involved a contrast between abstract lines and visual complexity. They illustrated this synthesis with Richard Neutra's Gill House in Glendale, California. In this work, "Neutra relied on the sweeping vistas… the room has become a clean reticent frame for the changing drama of the landscape, as well as a quiet background for life and thoughts."[5] Neutra, as one of the leading modernists at the time, represented a use of materials so refined and efficient that structure was clarified to the point of disappearing altogether. The subsequent demate-rialization of Neutra's design had allowed the site's natural landscape to be more present; the architecture, as *Interiors* implied, had become taciturn so that the dweller might think and the landscape might perform. Modernism, by exten-sion, was the means to bring together the austere forms from industrialized building production with the richness of landscape. Modernism was softened, or "gentled," in Jordy's terms, while outdoor scenery was telescoped, given greater depth for its contrast with evident artifice.
    A contrast between natural and abstract geometries was itself the visible manifestation of

— 4
Edgar Kaufmann Jr., *What is Modern Interior Design* (New York: Museum of Modern Art, 1953), p. 20.

— 5
Interiors (February 1947).

a more important dichotomy between nature and technology, which modern also managed to span. The perceived split between a technically rational-ized approach to the modern house, associated with functional planning, spare geometries, and packed with mechanical equipment and, in contrast, a romantic approach, which was characteristically associated with the presence of nature, defines the ideological spectrum within which residential design in the 1950s operated. Working exclusively at either extreme of the spectrum was fraught with risk of either alienation or irrelevance. But for the reasonably talented architect, the middle ground offered the best chances for success. It was suited to a clientele willing to take an aesthetic chance when buying automobiles, perhaps, but becoming risk averse when the stakes involved thirty or more years of mortgage payments.
    This attitude was made clear a few years later, in 1950, when editors at *Progressive Architecture* conducted their own review of the previous fifty years of architecture. Assessing the current architectural scene they found three distinct trends. The first they described as "a highly rationalized and ultra-refined direct statement of technic and purpose." The trend was the product of architects who exploited technological advances in the materials and methods of construction. The best exemplar of this mode was Mies van der Rohe and his plans for the campus of the Illinois Institute of Technology. At "the opposite end of the scale" was Frank Lloyd Wright's V. C. Morris Shop in San Francisco, a building characterized as "a highly personal romantic approach to organic architecture." Wright's shop stood for an American architectural tradition rooted in individual genius and the impulse to build in accordance with vital principles of nature. Admirable as either of these projects may have been on their own terms, they each represented extreme positions of either the technician or the romantic. Standing between these two peaks of architectural achievement and representing a more attainable path was San Francisco-based architect Albert Henry Hill's design for a private home in Ross, California. Hill's project was a "happy fusing" of the two extremes, neither anonymous nor too personal, technologi-cally up-to-date yet linked to landscape. The accompanying image of Hill's Dettner House is telling: wedged between a swath of sky and a wide

---

SHORT HISTORY OF ARCHITECTURE
cture is a shelter and a product of our skills. We change
tle, but we lose old skills and develop new one. Architec-
tisfies our permanent needs while using ever-changing
s. Also methods develop their own needs. Satisfying those
s recently confused with Architecture.

yal Wiesmann to Zvi Hecker:
e: About Mankind
nice to hear about Istanbul and that you are back… I liked
ell although during ten days of visit it never stopped
…
anks for your text… is that for Perspecta? Why not…
they are clever enough to see that beyond the seemingly
s critic there is a very poignant contemporary comment
.

From Rafi Segal to Perspecta 36:
Title: RE: 36 perspecta in response to the question on
"the idea of reconstruction of a territory that has been willfully
destroyed…"
So often we tend to associate the term re-construction or
construction with times of peace and prosperity, whereas
destruction is a direct result of war and conflict. The question
above to which I am responding assumes this as well, a progres-
sion from one to the other — first the destruction of war, then
construction, a sign of peace and stabilization. But as the Israeli-
Palestinian conflict vividly shows, destruction and construction
can no longer be regarded as opposite terms. Destruction is not
accidental (even without smart bombs), uncontrollable,
necessarily immediate; nor does construction always imply a
pre-conceived plan, an executed design from drawings to reality.
Both of these actions — equally significant interventions in the
built environment — are used, in so many creative ways, as means
of escalating conflict and engaging in war. Whether employed as

abrupt reactions to other violent events or as part of a long
term, slow, gradual process of transformation of the environment
– built and landscape.
    The current construction of the barrier, the wall in the West
Bank for example, is manifested at times in the actual building
of a wired fence, but essentially becomes a 150' wide "wipe out"
strip, cutting intentionally through villages, agricultural fields,
erasing houses, roads, olive plantations, etc. – a most effective
means of destruction through the apparent need for construction.
    This case might be too obvious and misleading, since here
an architectural element – a wall – is incorporated by the military as a form of fortification, becoming another component of a
tactical doctrine that demands a constant re-evaluation of the
limits and character of what could be regarded as a battlefield.
Yet in our work "A Civilian Occupation: the politics of Israeli
Architecture" (together with Eyal Weizman), war and architecture
are related in a completely different way. We do not refer to a
condition of war and it spatial outcomes, as executed within the

terrace, which together take up most of the image, is a house composed of only a broad flat roof echoing the terrace, a stone chimney, and a wall of glass.[6] Hill's design, which as a private home was the only example addressed to a middle-class market, was best suited for the majority of Americans. Modern in this case lay across the spectrum of contemporary design possibilities but its most promising avenue of acceptance was in the middle.

If it was middle-of-the-road, Hill's design was also the best of two worlds, the latest technology and the seemingly oldest heritage, landscape; it could illustrate a middle ground because it relied for visual effect on the contrast between, on the one hand, a set of forms that had come to signify modern methods of construction and functionalist planning – that is, "technic and purpose" – and, on the other hand, a natural setting. It was a machine-for-living in-the-garden. Functional planning so facilitated the owners' lives that they found themselves free to lounge in the splendid setting. Advanced technology, such as interior climate controls and a glass wall, had tamed nature enough that it might enter the home when the owners couldn't be outside. For its part, nature provided a stage on which technological forms might appear to heightened effect as well as a stunning back-drop for the occupants' daily life. In this example, middle modern was the lower ground upon which *Progressive Architecture* planted its flag.[7]

Another mediating strategy was to claim that modern forms were older than most people realized. This was the approach taken in 1950 by *House Beautiful*. In an issue dedicated to "the emerging American style," James Marston Fitch explained how the "new American architecture started 70 years ago" with the imposing figure of H. H. Richardson. It had proliferated since the 1880s through the countless decisions of anonymous architects and clients, all of whom insisted on the satisfaction of practical needs rather than stylistic conventions.[8] In her article "Prophet without Honor," Jean Murray Bangs, wife of architect Harwell Hamilton Harris, continued to show how the modern American house originated in the late-nineteenth century. After first considering Maybeck, she settled on the work of Greene and Greene, which included use of wood, an attention to practical details, and a premonitory use of glass:

—— 6
"American Architecture, 1900–1950," *Progressive Architecture* (January 1950), p. 103. Wright himself was frequently described as having synthesized opposites of, for example, "permanence and stability" with "movement, expansion and dispersal;" one was achieved with "solid block-like forms" and the other was seen with "far-flung appendages and distant vistas." In Vincent Scully, "The Heritage of Wright," *Zodiac*, no. 8 (1961), p. 9; cited in Robert Twombley, "Saving the Family: Middle Class Attraction to Wright's Prairie House, 1901–1909," *American Quarterly*, vol. 27, no. 1 (March 1975), pp. 57–72.

—— 7
Although the mediation of nature and technology is quite marked in American experience, it is by no means limited to it. German author Karl Selg, for instance, in a 1957 essay on "Single Family Houses," set up a similar scheme, describing three distinct developmental paths taken by modern architecture. Illustrated by the work of Mies, Gropius and Neutra, all three branches exhibited clear geo-metries and provided some sense of a larger landscape. In Mies's work, though, the right angle was the basis of a tectonic, more experimental, and perhaps more inward-looking architec-ture. For Gropius, clear geometry was an expedient, a convention of construction that facilitated the building task at hand. For Neutra, though, Selg thought the right angle was a metaphor. Rather than being an urban coordinate or having intrinsic interest, Neutra's use of strong geometries only heightened the experience of nature. In *Hand-buch Moderner Architektur* (1957).

—— 8
Fitch, "The New American Architecture Started 70 Years Ago," *House Beautiful*, vol. 92, no. 5 (May 1950), pp. 134–7.

Richard Neutra, Gill House. Glendale, California

Albert Henry Hill, Dettner House

Greene and Greene, Pratt House. Ojai, 1909

built environment by soldiers, tanks, machine guns, special forces, etc. Nor is this study focused around an account of the architecture of bunkers, barracks, military bases, fortifications, or structures constructed to serve the army in warfare. We rather term war through architecture as describing how territorial conflicts — national struggles over control on land — are played out through the most mundane typologies of architecture and urban planning. In the case of the Israeli-Palestinian conflict, we see that new towns, neighborhoods, and suburbs of the West Bank — civilian settlements — are used primarily as strategic weapons by the Israeli state to serve its geopolitical aims. Furthermore, what becomes evident (as Eyal Weizman clearly shows in the "Betzelm" map of Jewish Settlements of the West Bank), is that not only the mere location of settlements constitutes a breach of international law, but their specific form, shape and layout also inflicts, directly and indirectly, damage to the Palestinian population in terms of humanitarian rights, economy, urban growth, agriculture and land use, transportation, and

more. This emphasizes an elementary, most basic characteristic of architecture: of where when and how one builds — architec-ture's most intrinsic and essential features. We tend so often today to overlook this basic nature of the act of building.

Shouldn't such understandings of architecture be consis-tently addressed, not just through architectural critique but also in architectural education. Regardless of style, detailing, building materials, treatments of façades, innovative structural solutions (all important components of the profession), and preceding all these — other pressing issues should be at stake. In no way does this suggest a cruder or simplified interpretation of the architectural work, it plainly requires a different body of knowledge, a different sensitivity, a broader understanding of the context — urban, political, social — in which the power of archi-tecture is executed.

What we might find (within the role and responsibility of the architect) is that we need not only the knowledge of how to build, but also at times when and where not to.

Marcel Breuer, Wolfson House

The large glass areas in the new houses were anticipated by Greene and Greene, who used glass walls in the early 1900s. The dining room in the Blacker house in 1907 has windows on three sides of the room, and is divided by a sectional glass wall which can be folded back out of the way. The Crocker house in 1909, designed by Henry M. Greene, has a long gallery on the south, one wall of which is entirely of glass. In the Cordelia Culbertson house in 1911, the glass wall of the garden room can be made to disappear above the ceiling...[9]

In other words, glass walls in the 1950s were definitely something new; it was just that they had been new for a long time. Appreciated for generations without fanfare, they were already integrated into the everyday environment of the best houses. Along with other important characteristics of the "American Style," glass walls were so naturalized they had become invisible: "We have not been quick to recognize our new American Style because of its grass roots origin. Its very familiarity has made it hard to see, and made us take it for granted."[10] Innovation with the patina of tradition was the by-then assimilated amalgam already underfoot. The chief distinction between new architecture and old was the degree of self-awareness with which either was practiced. According to *House Beautiful*, what was lauded as modern in 1950 was presaged by nearly anonymous nineteenth-century vernacular architecture. What was old in this case wasn't just the landscape, essentialized as an eternal presence. Rather, it was the very habit of looking at the landscape through glass. In turn, outspoken modern architects were blinded by their pursuit of novelty from seeing how agreeably conventional their designs were. All that remained after this unveiling of the old in the new was the self-proclaimed modernist's strident rhetoric. Modernists were suddenly preaching to the choir they had first learned their sermon from. *House Beautiful*'s "New Conservatism" from 1955 – "we have absorbed the revolutions of the early 20th Century" – reiterated the completed assimilation of modernist design that had sprung up independently on American soil. Although nationalism was most blatant in the 1950s in *House Beautiful* under the editorial leadership of Elizabeth Gordon, its reliance on a strategy of mediating polarities, in this case old and new, was a discursive norm.[11]

Throughout the Fifties similar conceptual binaries were raised and then transcended specifically by modern architecture, especially in the sphere of residential design, where family harmony, along with women's labor, remained uncalculated and so was resistant to rationalization. Marcel Breuer, for example, described in 1948 the effects of one of his houses as combining the "sensation of man-made space, geometry and architecture... together with and in contrast to organic forms of nature and man." The "warm joy of security at the fireplace" contrasted with a modernist "drive toward experiment," which was evident in a thrilling glass-walled panorama. Both – an emotional quality and a quantifiable analytic – were essential to human experience and to modern design: "It is by the resolution of strong opposites that this house gains its character," he said.[12] Breuer's own influential "bi-nuclear" plan house,

—— 9
Bangs, "Prophet without Honor," *House Beautiful*, vol. 92, no. 5 (May 1950), pp. 138–9, 178–9. Bangs was instrumental in the new attention given Greene and Greene beginning in the late 1940s. Her article in *Architectural Forum* (October 1948) was cited when the regional AIA chapter gave a special award to the brothers. Mumford had perhaps initiated this effort in his writings on the Bay Area style.

—— 10
Elizabeth Gordon, "The New American Style Grew from America's Way of Life," *House Beautiful,* vol. 92, no. 5 (May 1950), p. 123.

—— 11
In "The New Conservatism," what was recently "modern" had by this time become a "tradition" and spoke of the "the new indoor-outdoor tradition." *House Beautiful* (April 1955), pp. 120–4, 224–6.

—— 12
Marcel Breuer cited in *Architectural Forum* (November 1948), p. 147, and in *Architectural Record* (February 1949), p. 85. Examples abound of modern architecture mediating these perceptual pairs: "Our house is extremely satisfying to live in. Pitched ceilings and glass walls somehow produce two opposite effects – snugness, spaciousness," reported the owner of a house designed by John Pekruhn, in "Pennsylvania House Balances a Way of Life," *Architectural Record* (mid-May 1956), pp. 189–91.

Marcel Breuer, Clark House

with its schematic division between an open living area and a more closed realm for sleeping and bathing, crystallized this sort of thinking, making modernism a mechanism of mediation between public and private, mind and body, as well as a contrast of cubic form with sylvan setting.

In some accounts, modernism had actually unleashed a previously repressed instinct for adventure and then integrated it into a balanced psychic economy. Elizabeth Mock was perhaps clearest in this regard. In a 1946 Museum of Modern Art publication on modern house design, Mock analyzed human instincts and found they held opposing spatial implications: on the one hand, security, which required a firm enclosure, and on the other hand a sense of personal freedom, for which nothing but open space would do. In providing secure shelter, traditional architecture had inevitably to compromise an instinctual yearning for open space. But the sum of human experience, Mock implied, involved a balance of opposites:

> A thesis exists only in relation to its antithesis: light needs darkness, bigness needs smallness, freedom needs constraint and good can be pursued only in the knowledge of evil. Man retains his primitive need for cave-like security even while he delights in unlimited light and space, and the best modern houses give both.

Only modern architecture was able to coordinate the opposites of prospect and refuge simultaneously. Arguments regarding modernism's efficient means of construction remained relevant, but turned here to satisfying the web of human instinct. Despite her willingness to consider all sides of human psychology, that is, both of them, Mock mapped developmental and moral correlates onto her architectural and perceptual dichotomy. In other words, seeking a strong sense of enclosure was perfectly acceptable, that is, for those ready to admit their own Neanderthal insecurities and their cravings for darkness, smallness, constraint, and evil.13

Eero Saarinen, to cite another example, also thought at the end of the 1950s that formal opposition descended directly from binary mental states that were innate. Literally equating a sense of openness with consciousness, or at least wakefulness, Saarinen described the house he hoped one day to build for himself: "The only logical kind would have two floors, a glass box above ground and a windowless box below ground. For a bedroom you need only a dark cave."14 A modern house brought opposite poles together yet by reinforcing one another through contrast allowed each pole to remain true to its own essence. Modernism's interior openness was only half the story, architects claimed; privacy, too, was improved with modern architecture. Architecture, always a practice only partly autonomous from social circumstance, aimed in postwar America toward this middle ground between social and formal extremes.

Finding tensions between nature and technology is a hallmark of American imaginative and, thus, historical experience. The terms have proven over time to be more symbiotic than exclusive. Leo Marx in 1964 described the mutual contribution of both nature and technology to the longstanding

15 ——
See *The Machine in the Garden* (Oxford: Oxford University Press, 1964), p. 6; Howard Segal, *Technological Utopianism in American Culture* (Chicago: University of Chicago Press, 1985), p. 24. Suburbs, for example, were often explained as the "golden means" between city and country. See F. L. Olmsted, *Riverside in 1871, with a Description of Its Improvements* (1871), p. 21.

13 ——
Elizabeth Mock, *If You Want to Build a House* (New York, 1946), p. 42. Mock was far from alone, however, as contemporary writers and later historians have identified a primitivism in modern experience counterbalanced by more progressive attributes. In architectural writing this dichotomy takes on spatial form and perceptual character. See, for example, Matei Calinescu regarding modern literature in *Five Faces of Modernity* (Durham: Duke University Press, 1987); T. J. Lears regarding American history in *No Place of Grace: Antimodernism and the Transformation of American Culture 1880–1920* (New York: Pantheon, 1981). Compare also Sigfried Giedion on Wright. Giedion thought that Wright's "cautiousness" and "hesitation about opening up the house with glass walls" was due to his understanding of "the human animal" as a creature with "primitive eternal instincts" and a "desire for shadowed dimness" that could, Giedion hints, be an artifact of "his generation," which, on occasion, he had to overcome. In *Space, Time and Architecture* [1941], 5th edition (Cambridge, Mass.: Harvard University Press, 1967), p. 417.

16 ——
Architectural Forum (November 1948), p. 145. Hans Huth thought that the call to nature was pervasive during the 1950s: "No power could ever divert the increasing support public opinion is giving to the idea of bringing nature and man into a harmonious relationship." In Hans Huth, *Nature and the American: Three Centuries of Changing Attitudes* (Berkeley: University California Press, 1957), p. 4. That one of the lessons of World War II was the appropriateness of modern architecture was widespread. For example: "Perhaps a citizenry just recovered from the second world war and already threatened by a third has decided that quaint green shutters are something less than an adequate defense against the atomic bomb. Perhaps inflation and television are keeping families at home and they are beginning to realize the defects of their closed-in boxes." In "The Cape Cod Cottage," *Architectural Forum* (February 1949), pp. 89–93, and *Architectural Forum* (March 1949), pp. 101–6.

14 ——
In "Houses Architects Live In," *Life*, vol. 46, no. 3 (19 January 1959), p. 55.

literary trope he named "complex pastoralism." Getting "closer to nature," at any stage of society, Marx observed, is "the psychic root of all pastoralism – genuine and spurious." The "machine in the garden" remains a vivid and enduring image of these competing impulses. Besides finding them, resolving tensions between nature and technology also is a hallmark of American thinking. Howard Segal argues that in utopian thought these allegedly opposing forces may find a common meeting ground, a place where both are compatible but neither is compromised: "The envisioned domestication of both technology and nature will resolve the tension that Leo Marx, among others, has deemed irresolvable: the tension between the industrial and agrarian orders, between the machine and the garden that Marx believes lies at the heart of the American experience."15

In the aftermath of World War II, another reason to seek shelter in nature may be seen as well. As if any further proof were needed, technology had displayed during wartime its dark side. Widely evident at the beginning of the Cold War, architectural literature also reflected a new anxiety regarding technology. "Only within the last few years has the terrible question of the machine been put in terms awesome enough to produce a general realization of the crisis of man," ran an argument in a special issue of *Architectural Forum*. The issue attempted to summarize the increasingly technical knowledge essential to the contemporary practice of architecture. Architecture was inescapably bound to "collaborate truly with technology," but it must avoid the "technologist's approach," which had been a partner to global warfare. Even short of physical destruction, this technologically-induced crisis posed a constant threat to the mind as well. The awesome forces released by technological progress had precipitated a state of psychic emergency. Spiritual well-being required of the architect more than simply the "mechanical satisfaction" of physical needs, however indispensable that might ultimately be. Editors at *Forum* believed the architect, as shaper of the built environment, was in a unique position to effect a remedy, being "the one force capable of generating a reversal of the continuing alienation of man from himself." "What can we do to retrieve our lost sensibilities?" they wondered aloud.16

If sensibilities went lost in an artificial world, then a conceptual symmetry endemic to the period demanded they be retrieved in a natural world. In many instances, a renewed desire for nature was the direct result of the rapid march of mechanization. At a time when "suburban man" spent most "of his day in an artificial atmosphere," it fell to the architect, "whose job is to create man's immediate physical environment," to make a place to comfort the body and delight the mind. In architectural terms this meant relating "the building to the land, machine forms to the forms of nature." Though vague, the formula presented no theoretical difficulties: "There does not seem to be the fundamental conflict between the forms of technology and the forms of nature that categorical thinking would lead us to believe." More than this, advanced technology actually necessitated renewed relations with nature. "On the one hand, the complex demands of modern life dictate the most precise and scientific manipulation of building. On the other, increasing mechanization seems to have awakened a new longing for nature which has to be met in building."[17] Ideologically bound to the narratives of technological advance that were present at its inception and promoted in its early histories, modern architecture reached out increasingly to nature in an attempt to bring the two together. Modern architecture effectively promised to incrementalize technological progress, that is, to ratchet modernity into the human life that preceded it, and to do so gradually rather than cataclysmically.

Concealment: literal

We forget how glass panes have so greatly extended our control over the world by allowing us to see it in comfort.[18] Yi-Fu Tuan

The mediation of opposites could not simply be stated; to be convincing it had to be made visible in distinctly architectural terms. A middle modern had meaning only if it made its mediation manifest, and it was able to do so by emphasizing the effects of technologies rather than the technologies themselves. That is to say that modernism's commitment to the aesthetic revelation of its means is evident in their disappearance. Transparency was at this point reappraised in modern architecture for its ability to connect modern citizens both with the outdoors and with their own inner natures and invisibility became visible proof of modernism's continued claims of a relevance beyond style. In fact, transparency is consistent with the way many technological artifacts work, including architecture. In his philosophy of technology, Albert Borgmann distinguishes the "commodity" of technology, that is, the benefit it confers, from the "device" or machinery that produces that benefit. He mentions television as an example, which is valued for the picture it presents and not at all for how that picture got there. Borgmann names this condition the "device paradigm": "What distinguishes a device is its sharp internal division into a machinery and a commodity procured by that machinery." The technological means are subordinated to the achievement of an effect, product, or service. Borgmann suggests that this division is related to consumer society, specifically "the consumption of those central commodities which constitute the foremost and final aspect of technology." From the beneficiary's, or consumer's point of view, how something gets done is uninteresting. If anything, Borgmann notes that, to the seemingly "commodious" delivery of such benefits, "there corresponds an extreme concealment or abstractness in the mode of its production." If anything, consumer society sharpens the split between the commodity and the mechanism that produces it. Progress in technology – and a technologically-based architecture – may in this way be measured by its disappearance or dematerialization. As a result, advancing technology leaves in its wake a growing gap between diminished means and amplified ends. As Borgmann puts it, "The peculiar presence of the end of the device is made possible by means of the device and its concealment."[19] For

—— 17
Architectural Forum (November 1948), pp. 91, 146–7. Compare also, Edgar Kaufmann, Jr., *What is Modern Interior Design?* (New York: Museum of Modern Art, 1953), p. 18.

—— 18
Yi-Fu Tuan, *Topophilia* (1974), p. 181.

20 ——
Architectural Record, vol. 105, no. 6 (June 1949), pp. 96–101.

21 ——
House and Garden (December 1948), pp. 13–33.
—— 19
Albert Borgmann, *Technology and the Character of Contemporary Life: A Philosophical Inquiry* (Chicago: University of Chicago Press, 1984), p. 33. To borrow historian of technology Peter McCleary's terms, the "amplification" of nature required a parallel "reduction" of technological artifice. See Peter McCleary, "Some Characteristics of a New Concept of Technology," *Journal of Architectural Education*, vol. 42, no. 1 (Fall 1988), pp. 2–9, 125, 48.

much postwar modernism, a strategy of concealment involved uncoupling architectural effects from the mechanism of their production and then reconfiguring those effects within a preferred hierarchy of values. Concealment was the necessary but unseen strategy that made transparency work. Technology was made present by hiding its physical mechanisms while displaying its effects. This was less a matter of the actual use of specific technologies than the degree to which they were registered in the visual environment. Concealment operated at a variety of scales to emphasize the experience of nature rather than the knowledge of technology.

At the scale of the site, architects removed from view evidence of a larger urban system while providing at the same time all the benefits to be drawn from urban infrastructure. The home site was conceived as an encounter between the deeply personal act of dwelling and all the technological improvements that facilitated dwelling, which included not only mechanical systems in the home but also earth-moving equipment, power lines, roads, sewer lines, legal instruments like deeds, financial instruments like mortgages, intermediaries like real estate brokers who brought together buyers and sellers, even anxieties about resale value that influenced buyers' site preferences in the first place. The visible presence of technological mediation would, many believed, diminish the purposes served by the dwelling. This was the core argument of Neutra's 1951 *Mystery and Realities of the Site*, for instance, whose title summarized the contrast between an unfathomable nature – a singular mystery – and the bureaucratic approach to creating environment – the plural realities.

In "Designing What Comes Naturally," *Architectural Record* considered another more widely published house by Henry Hill. The article assured readers that the natural quality of the house, "while readily seen in the photographs, tends to grow more impressive as one begins to appreciate the scale of the house and its glass areas and views."[20] The view, in a sense, augmented the photogenic as much as it was represented photographically. When the same house was published by *House and Garden* several months earlier, after receiving a second prize in the magazine's "Awards in Architecture," it was contrasted with the nineteenth-century Spreckels Mansion, which was merely sketched, on Nob Hill in San Francisco, in an article called "Old Houses vs. New Homes." Old houses, "with their boarded, sightless windows," the article argued, were in decline because they just couldn't take advantage of the site the way that modern houses could because modernism mediated "country living and city convenience." While conceding that the Spreckels Mansion "curves lofty windows to the view" of the cityscape, Hill's design for Mr. and Mrs. Sidney Herspring oriented the entire house to the outlook. The main living areas "are dominated by a view of Mt. Tamalpais."[21] In *Record*'s subsequent coverage, and elsewhere, the modern house was referred to simply by the name of its view: "Tamalpais House."

The encounter between nature and artifice was evident, too, in the theme of commuting, where it had been addressed at least since the early nineteenth century.[22] In the twentieth century modern houses were frequently described as being convenient to the jobs and cultural amenities of a city but were depicted in an uninhabited, apparently remote landscape. Proximity was registered by a word or two regarding the commute. Architect Edgar Tafel's house, for instance, was located on "a deceptively rural site," the "major asset" of which was its view. The deception was due to the fact that, while it looked remote, the house was "within commuting distance of Manhattan."[23] But for the brief mention, the commute is, literally, hidden from view. Especially after World War II, commuting became a subgenre of suburban criticism that nevertheless indicated a certain degree of status.[24] Comfort in the car during the commute then became a prominent theme of automobile manufacturers. While easy commutes were part of the appeal of a sub- or ex-urban house, the convenient hours spent behind the wheel in traffic each day tended not to be illustrated. If anything, comfortable daily commutes to remote sites were taken to be just another facet of technologically-enhanced modern life. In 1951 they were hardly considered visionary: "it is no longer starry-eyed to envision a middle-income family having a country home which still allows the wage-earner to commute a hundred miles distance each day with ease."[25] Commuting, in other words, registered the presence of the city but rendered it in terms of unseen time spent enjoying the drive in relative comfort, akin to sitting in the living-room easy chair and enjoying a landscape view.

At the scale of the house itself, connections with both city and nature resulted in a formal split. Rooms with dedicated functions, like garages and kitchens, migrated to the front of the house while unprogrammed living areas moved toward the rear, that is, away from the street. A number of modern houses were built that eschewed civic gestures altogether and concentrated instead on the private rear of the house. Craig Ellwood's design for a house in Los Angeles, for instance, featured "a relatively closed face to the street and a completely open side to the lawn and vistas to the rear."[26] A further development of Wright's "Queen Anne front, Mary Anne behind," houses were described in the '50s as being schizophrenic. *Architectural Forum*'s review of "A House Divided" described a design that was traditional looking from the street, indicated mostly by small windows, but was modern on the inside, largely by virtue of its glass walls overlooking the rear yard. The design said to the editors that modern architecture was a good place to look out from but not to look at. The link between a schizophrenic house and the psychic state of its occupants was made readily apparent to readers. In a rebuttal, the architect, Rene Travelletti, argued that any schizophrenia would be due more to the occupants' "nudism," that is, to exposing their home life to the street, than to the design itself.[27] Robert Woods Kennedy noted that some clients actually demanded a "traditional front, modern behind."[28] By 1958, *Sunset* described a blank façade facing the street as itself a "venerable custom."[29] At this scale, and in regard to accusations of schizophrenic form, modern was less in the middle than it was one-half of a whole. To the degree that the street was portrayed as crowded or unkempt a private landscape view was

—— 22
See, for example, Sam Bass Warner, *Streetcar Suburbs* (Cambridge, Mass.: Harvard University Press, 1962); Henry Binford, *The First Suburbs: Residential Communities on the Boston Periphery 1815–1860* (Chicago: University of Chicago Press, 1985); Kenneth Jackson, *Crabgrass Frontier* (New York: Oxford University Press, 1985).

—— 23
"Tafel Residence," *Architectural Forum* (August 1948), p. 78.

—— 24
See, for example, C. Morgan, "Commuter's Club," *Christian Science Monitor Weekly* (July 8, 1944), p. 5, and H. H. Smith, "Gosh, I Envy Commuters!," *Saturday Evening Post,* vol. 226 (26 June 1954), pp. 30ff. Length of commute as indication of status is discussed in *Fortune* (May 1959), p. 109. Downing had already remarked on the custom of commuting as the practice of extracting economic means in the city to enjoy the country. See "Hints to Rural Improvers," *Rural Essays* (New York: Leavitt, Allen, 1857), p. 111, and the discussion in Peter Schmitt, *Back to Nature* (Baltimore: Johns Hopkins University Press, 1969), pp. 5–6.
—— 25
Paul Lazlo, "The House of the Future," *Fortnight* (24 December 1951), p. 16.

—— 26
"West LA, California," in special issue on "The Private House," *Progressive Architecture,* vol. 36, no. 5 (May 1955), p. 116.

—— 27
Architectural Forum (June 1948), pp. 110–3.
—— 28
Robert Woods Kennedy, *The House and the Art of Its Design* (New York: Reinhold, 1953), p. 386. This was a common theme: "House with Two Faces in a Suburb," in Jean and Don Graf, *Practical Houses for Contemporary Living* (New York: Dodge, 1953), pp. 78–9; "How to Flop Over a Wrong-Way House," *House and Home,* vol. 6, no. 4 (October 1954), pp. 140–3, as well as "A House Divided," *Architectural Forum* (June 1948), pp. 110–3, mentioned above.
—— 29
"Western Ranch Houses by Cliff May," *Sunset Magazine* (Menlo Park, Calif.: Lane, 1958), p. 14.

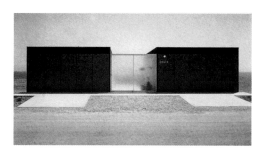

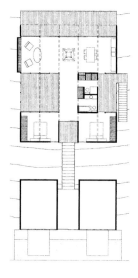

Craig Ellwood's design for a house in Los Angeles: exterior, façade, plan and interior

Michael Wesely and Lina Kim
From the series *Brasilia*
2003

unpopulated and visually whole. If the street signified anonymity, anomie, and the loss of autonomy, then a modest green view seemed to prove the private realm was essentially intact. In short, even a humble backyard view compensated for modern life by imaginatively reconstructing a landscape urban society had already overrun.

Once the balance between nature and technology had been tipped in this way, even discussions of new building systems came to be justified in part by their ability to disappear. One of the most promising aspects of the "Post-Beam-Plank" construction, to name only one example, discussed by *House and Home* in June 1954, was that the system easily accommodated large sheets of glass, resulting in "a merger of indoor and outdoor spaces, which makes the indoors look much bigger than it really is." The legitimacy of the construction was its contribution to an illusion.[30] Homeowners were invited to think of their home site as a matrix of appearances and the architect as an expert in opening or closing visual channels along a grid that will result in a unique pattern of visibility. "See what you can see from the place," counseled Neutra; imagine then how to screen out the man-made in favor of nature.[31]

Concealment is evident too at the scale of individual elements of architecture, with no feature embodying the contest between nature and technology so well as a glass wall. Glass walls were a leading index of modern design and when bundled with a view they were proof of proximity to nature. Glass walls remained evidence of sophisticated building practices, requiring wide openings, transport to an often isolated site, precise dimensional tolerances and great care during construction, not to mention the sensitive control systems needed to offset greater temperature fluctuations induced by glass walls. Though the glass wall stood out as a technological feature, it seemed to disappear visually. In this way it seemed almost to step aside of its own accord in order to fulfill its primary purpose, intimacy with nature. It functioned simultaneously as a register of modern construction and nearness to nature, joining both ends of the romantic-technic scale from which *Progressive Architecture* got its architectural bearings. Initially a technological proposition, the glass wall had become a therapeutic imperative. In short, glass was a stunning technological achievement but its true imaginative potency lay in its transparency; a leading sign of architectural skill was nearly invisible. It resonated as both an advance in engineering artifice and a return to natural virtues: "The use of large glass areas which gives modern architecture its unique quality of spaciousness and kinship with the out-of-doors is inseparably linked with such technological advances as double glazing and related thermal controls."[32] A view of landscape was the primary sign that the technology of glass wall construction was "working." A view was a kind of dial tone announcing that the vast unseen infrastructure was on.

In this way, glass walls were also a topos of inbetween. *House and Home*'s 1952 "traditional house in the modern idiom," for example, balanced "classical discipline and modern, technological freedom." Modern use of glass was in the middle not simply because it simultaneously joined and

33 ——
Referring to houses in New Canaan, Connecticut, by Breuer, Johnson, and Johansen. *House and Home* (January 1952), pp. 108–9.

—— 30
"Post-Beam-Plank Construction," *House and Home,* vol. 5, no. 6 (June 1954), p. 98.
34 ——
In *Better Homes and Gardens* (1953).

—— 31
Neutra (1951), op. cit., p. 62.

35 ——
"From its wall of glass, framing a view to the South, *to the Bryant Boiler that activates its unseen radiant coils*, it is as modern as tomorrow" and located in architect Robert Vahlberg's "Dream House" in Oklahoma City. In Bryant Automatic Heating of Affiliated Gas Equipment, Inc. Cleveland, advertisement, *Architectural Forum* (March 1949), p. 55; Bell Telephone System, advertisement, *National Real Estate and Building Journal*, vol. 52, no. 1 (January 1951), n.p.; Lawrence Kocher, "The New House for Family Living," *Architectural Record*, vol. 119, no. 6 (mid-May 1956), p. 101.
—— 32
Architectural Forum (November 1948), p. 140.

36 ——
Reyner Banham in his chapter on "Concealed Power" in *The Architecture of the Well-Tempered Environment* (London: Architectural Press, 1969).

separated inside and out, but also because it indicated, on the one hand, "the technology of our time," while on the other hand, inviting inside the sweeping dimensions of landscape. Proffering thereby a monumental scale, glass walls could suggest the "permanence of 'home'" rather than the "temporariness of 'industrialized shelter.'"[33] In issue after issue, in journal after journal, from popular to professional, modern walls of glass were literally poised inbetween inside and out, making possible the most enduring cliche of the period: to bring the outdoors indoors.

Even at the level of mechanical equipment, technological traits were downplayed in order to heighten the presence of nature. Invisibility was an explicit advantage stressed by manufacturers. The somatic benefit of Crane Heating's furnace was comfort in a range of climatic conditions, from hot summer to cold winter; the visual benefit was a natural scene. The physical comfort provided by mechanical specialties was represented as a picture of nature.[34] In this sense, the landscape was a conjecture of the mechanism. In an advertisement for Uskon radiant heat, a swirling snowstorm appeared behind the picture window to enliven an evening party. The copy read: "No furnace, no pipes, no fuel storage. No ashes, dirt or dust. No radiators. Uskon is 'invisible.'" The product was promoted for its ability to disappear. Nature's inhospitability became a party ornament and was gauged, if at all, in terms of a seasonal expense for heating. Uskon proposed an apparently unmediated relation to the outside by emphasizing the invisibility of the technology the dweller was so bodily intimate with, so dependent on, and yet remained for that user largely alien and incomprehensible. Other examples abound: Bell Telephone System suggested architects "Plan 'a disappearing act' for telephone wires" by hiding them within walls or above ceilings; a special issue of *Architectural Record* reported experiments that replaced window insect screening with invisible "periodical applications of insect repelling spray around the house" that would add nothing to the feeling of enclosure.[35] Although conceptually available for traditional styles of architecture, the mediation of nature and technology had by the 1950s been effectively appropriated by modern architecture.

For the average citizen, the device paradigm, discernable at different scales in modern architecture, entails a kind of magic in the tenuous and obscure connection between ends and means. A bit of magic, or mystification, is not unknown in the history of domestic architecture but it is surprising to find such sustained interest in concealment in an architecture founded, at least in part, on efforts to render its means of making manifest. Reyner Banham suggested as much at the close of the 1960s. A troublesome historiographical problem as well as an internal contradiction were the result of certain "concealments," as he put it, that were discernable within a modernist aesthetic otherwise "conspicuously given to honest exhibition of structures and services."[36] It may be due as much to Borgman's "device paradigm" as to the very genre of view. As Rosalind Krauss defines it, "*view* addresses a notion of authorship in which the natural phenomenon, the point of interest, rises up to confront the viewer, seemingly without the mediation of an individual recorder or artist."[37] To the extent that modern architecture capitalized on its ability to provide views through walls of glass, it contributed to this mystification. The landscape appears self-organized when the framing apparatus is disregarded. But it may also have to do with an attempt on the part of professionals to appeal to the peculiarities of the postwar marketplace for their services. Few were quite as candid as Robert Woods Kennedy when he said that in architecture as in magic itself "the absolute secrecy of the trick is the essence." In the push-button ethos of the postwar period, providing effects without awakening clients' understanding of the technology behind those effects was central, whether in regard to a television, a car, or a house. Aesthetic impact was enhanced, many believed, when rational inquiry slept. Though perhaps overstating the case, Kennedy clarified the polarity: "In architecture, the architect who leaves us mystified, who excites us with an invisible technique, is the most rewarding. To allow one's slip to show, be it silk, steel, or Freudian is, because it spoils the show, the unforgivable, unprofessional, inartistic sin."[38] A middle modern, then, was predicated on concealment and its art was gratifying for its seemingly effortless delivery of physical and visual benefits. Middle modern did not refuse new technologies in the home so much as it welcomed them as a spectacle of disappearance.

Modern without a middle

> ... only the middleground of an argument is of use...[39] Colin Rowe and Fred Koetter

An experience of transparency to landscape enhanced by a corresponding concealment of artifice contributes nothing to knowledge regarding the intersections of nature and humankind. More likely, it obscures such knowledge, which is part of transparency's appeal: its crystalline delight is a distraction from what Adorno and Horkheimer called in 1944 "the labor of conceptualization": "False clarity is only another name for myth; and myth has always been obscure and enlightening at one and the same time: always using the devices of familiarity and straightforward dismissal to avoid the labor of conceptualization."[40] Mystification, for the two writers, involves the attempt to render current practices in terms of "mythic process," that is, to make "the new appear as the predetermined, which is accordingly the old." Specifically, rendering complex physical and social technologies in pictorial terms flattens them, or, as they put it, "appropriates and perpetuates existence as a schema." In other words, the device paradigm that guided much postwar architecture was a means of selectively reconfiguring perceptual attributes of the built environment to generate a setting conducive to cultural fantasies. To the extent that the selection of exterior phenomena for representation within a building can be delegated to the properties of an autonomous system or unseen processes, it becomes less an aesthetic option than an axiom, acquiring along the way some of the functions of ideology. The more the formula is repeated without criticism, the more it

—— 37
In "Photography's Discursive Spaces," *The Originality of the Avant-Garde and Other Modernist Myths* (Cambridge, Mass.: MIT Press, 1985), p. 140.

41 ——
Henry James, *The American Scene.*

42 ——
"Windows and Gardens" [1954], *From the Ground Up* (New York: Harvest, 1956), pp. 184–5.

—— 38
In *The House and the Art of Its Design* (New York: Reinhold, 1953) p. 527.

—— 39
Rowe and Koetter, *Collage City* (Cambridge, Mass.: MIT Press, 1978), p. 49.

—— 40
Dialectic of Enlightenment [1944] (New York: Continuum), p. xiv.

is taken as a simple truth and the more the benefits of transparency can be savored without conceptual difficulties. The most succinct statement of precisely this cycle was given by Henry James in 1907: "When you wander about in Arcadia you ask as few questions as possible. That *is* Arcadia in fact."[41]

Disenchantment with unbridled consumerism along with a dawning awareness of the geographical homogenization resulting from it began in the 1960s to affect mainstream architectural thinking. With civil rights and women's movements, youth culture and the stirrings of environmentalism, formerly disenfranchised groups and obscure aspects of society came sharply and suddenly into focus. Modernism's reliance on formal traits like transparency likewise came to be seen as an unsupportable "opaque passion," as Mumford had already said in 1954.[42] Embraced in the postwar period, modern architecture had also gotten enmeshed with that period's larger scale of urban development and associated with the interests of an often rapacious marketplace and the nation's more global ambitions. With urban renewal money in the 1960s supporting well-publicized housing projects, modern architecture was witnessed devouring city centers and picking at overseas opportunities, and over the course of the decade collapsed from its own weight. With the loss of consensus regarding modernism, its mediating posture was likewise abandoned. Some architects began explicitly to embrace opposing ideological poles, evident for instance in the early work of Venturi, the New York Five, and the White and Gray debates of the early 1970s. However related in their responses to a preceding modernism, these later positions emphasized their incompatibility, their resistance to mediation. The alleged success or failure of former modernisms was remedied by a one-sided development either of unexplored formal potential or popular legibility. Although, in fact, a flexible line, the difference between a self-reflexive aesthetic withdrawal and a willing surrender to the commercial vernacular was widened once middle modern of the postwar era dropped out of sight. The critical journal *Oppositions* was, according to its founders, predicated on the loss of a consensual middle ground. With its demise, "modern" had itself become an absent middle from which theoretical viewpoints diverged.

THE CITY: LOCALIZATIONS OF THE GLOBAL

SASKIA SASSEN

1 ⸺
Also new – though not the focus in this article – is the growing use of digital networks by often poor neighborhood organizations to pursue a variety of both intra- and inter-urban political initiatives. All of this has raised the number of cities that are part of cross-border networks operating at often vast geographic scales.

Over the centuries cities have been at the intersection of processes with supra-urban and even intercontinental scales. What is different today is the intensity, complexity and global span of these networks, and the extent to which significant portions of economies are now dematerialized and digitized and hence can travel at great speeds through these networks where before they were fixed in place.[1]

As cities and urban regions are increasingly traversed by non-local circuits, much of what we experience as the local is also global because the local is actually a transformed condition, a localization of global processes. One way of thinking about this is in terms of urban processes and entities in cities. These might be economic, political, cultural, or imaginary. This produces a specific set of interactions in a city's relation to its topography. The topographic representation of the city can capture only some of this, and further, even if captured, will tend to represent it as contained within the city when it might in fact be a spatialization of a trans-urban process.

The new urban spatiality thus produced is partial in a double sense: it accounts for only part of what happens in cities and what cities are about, and it inhabits only part of what we might think of as the space of the city, whether this be understood in terms as diverse as those of a city's administrative boundaries or in the sense of the multiple public imaginaries that may be present in different sectors of a city's people.

This raises a number of questions. Let me address two in this short essay. One is the question of place: what is urban place in this context? The other concerns the resulting repositioning of architecture, planning, and urbanism generally, as forms of knowledge and forms of practice.

Sited materialities and global span

I want to address the question of place in today's cities through the lens of the digital global economy.

It seems to me that the difficulty analysts and commentators have had specifying/understanding the impact of digitization on cities – indeed, on multiple configurations – essentially results from two analytic flaws. One of these (especially evident in the U.S.) confines interpretation to a technological reading of the technical capabilities of digital technology. This is fine for engineers. But such a reading becomes problematic when we want to understand how these technologies interact with social conditions, notably place. A purely technological reading of technical capabilities of digital technology inevitably leads one to a place that is a non-place, where we can announce with certainty the neutralizing of many of the configurations marked by physicality and place-boundedness, such as the urban.[2]

The second flaw, I would argue, is a continuing reliance on analytical categories that were developed under other spatial and historical conditions, that is, conditions preceding the current digital era. Thus the tendency is to conceive of the digital as simply and exclusively digital and the non-digital (whether represented in terms of the physical/material or the actual, all problematic though common conceptions) as simply and exclusively that, non-digital. These either/or categorizations filter out the possibility of mediating conditions, thereby precluding a more complex reading of the impact of digitization on material and place-bound conditions.

An alternative categorization would capture imbrications between the digital and the non-digital. Let me illustrate this using the case of finance. Finance is certainly a highly digitized activity; yet it cannot be thought of as exclusively digital. To have electronic financial markets and digitized financial instruments requires enormous amounts of materiel, not to mention human talent (which has its own type of physicality). This materiel includes conventional infrastructure, buildings, airports, and so on. Much of this materiel is, then, inflected by the digital. Obversely, much of what takes place in cyberspace is deeply inflected by the cultures, the material practices, the imaginaries, that take place outside cyberspace. Much, though not all, of what we think of when it comes to cyberspace would lack any meaning or referents if we were to exclude the world outside cyberspace. In brief, digital space and digitization are not exclusive conditions that stand outside the non-digital. Digital space is embedded in the larger societal, cultural, subjective, economic, imaginary structures of lived experience and the systems within which we exist and operate.[3]

The complex imbrications between the digital (as well as the global) and the non-digital brings with it a destabilizing of older hierarchies of scale and often dramatic re-scalings. As the national scale loses significance along

⸺ **2**
Another consequence of this type of reading is to assume that a new technology will *ipso facto* replace all older technologies that are less efficient, or slower, at executing the tasks the new technology is best at. We know that historically this is not the case. For a variety of critical examinations of the tendency towards technological determinism in much of the social sciences today, see the special issue of *Current Sociology* on "The Social World in the 21st Century: Ambivalent Legacies and Rising Challenges of Technologies," ed. Judy Wajcman, vol. 50, no. 3 (May 2002).

3 ⸺
Please see "Digital Networks and Power," M. Featherstone and S. Lash (eds.), *Spaces of Culture: City, Nation, World* (London: Sage, 1999), pp. 49–63.

with the loss of key components of the national state's formal authority over the national scale, other scales gain strategic importance. Most especially among these are sub-national scales such as the global city, and supra-national scales such as global markets or regional trading zones. Older hierarchies of scale (emerging in the historical context of the ascendance of the nation-state), which continue to operate, are typically organized in terms of institutional size: from the international, down to the national, the regional, the urban, down to the local. Today's re-scaling cuts across institutional size and, through policies such as deregulation and privatization, cuts across the institutional encasements of territory produced by the formation of national states. This does not mean that the old hierarchies disappear, but rather that re-scalings emerge alongside the old ones, and that they can often trump the latter.

These transformations which continue to entail complex imbrications of the digital and non-digital and between the global and the non-global, can be captured in a variety of instances. For example, much of what we might still experience as the "local" (an office building or a house or an institution right there in our neighborhood or downtown) actually is something I would rather think of as a "microenvironment with global span" insofar as it is deeply inter-networked. Such a microenvironment is in many senses a localized entity, something that can be experienced as local, immediate, proximate and hence captured in topographic representations. It is a sited materiality. But it is also part of global digital networks which give it immediate far-flung span. To continue to think of this as simply local is neither useful nor adequate. More importantly, the juxtaposition of a sited materiality and a global span, captures the imbrication of the digital in the non-digital and illustrates the inadequacy of a purely technological reading of the technical capacities of digitization. It also illustrates the inadequacy of a purely topographical reading.

A second example is the bundle of conditions and dynamics that marks the model of the global city. Just to single out one key dynamic: the more globalized and digitized the operations of firms and markets, the more their central management and coordination functions (and the requisite material structures) become strategic. It is precisely because of digitization that simultaneous worldwide dispersal of operations (whether factories, offices, or service outlets) and system integration can be achieved. And it is precisely this combination which raises the importance of central functions. Global cities are strategic sites for the combination of resources necessary for the production of these central functions.[4]

Much of what is liquefied and circulates in digital networks and is marked by hyper-mobility, remains physical in some of its components. Take, for example, real estate. Financial services firms have invented instruments that liquefy real estate, thereby facilitating investment and circulation of these instruments in global markets. Yet, part of what constitutes real estate remains very physical. At the same time, however, that which remains physical has been transformed by the fact that it is represented by highly liquid instruments that can circulate in global markets. It may look the same, it may involve the same bricks and mortar, it may be new or old, but it is a trans-formed entity.

We have difficulty capturing this multi-valence through our conventional categories: if it is physical, it is physical; and if it is digital, it is digital. In fact, the partial representation of real estate through liquid financial instruments produces a complex imbrication of the material and the de-materialized moments of that which we continue to call real estate. And it is precisely because of the digital capabilities of the economic sectors represented in global cities that the massive concentrations of material resources in these cities exist and keep expanding.

Hyper-mobility and de-materialization are usually seen as mere functions of the new technologies. This understanding erases the fact that it takes multiple material conditions to achieve this outcome and that it takes social networks not only digital ones.[5]

Once we recognize that the hyper-mobility of the instrument, or the de-materialization of the actual piece of real estate, had to be produced, we introduce the imbrication of the material and the non-material. It takes capital fixity to produce capital mobility, that is to say, state-of-the-art built environ-ments, conventional infrastructure – from highways to airports and railways – and well-housed talent. These are all, at least partly place-bound conditions, even though the nature of their place-boundedness is going to be different from what it was 100 years ago, when place-boundedness was much closer to pure immobility. Today it is a place-boundedness that is inflected, inscribed,

4 ——
These economic global city functions are to be distinguished from political global city func-tions, which might include the politics of contestation by formal and informal political actors enabled by these economic func-tions. This particular form of political global city functions is, then, in a dialectical relation (both enabled and in opposition) to the economic functions. See S. Sassen, "New Frontiers Facing Urban Sociology," *British Journal of Sociology*, vol. 51, no. 1 (January/March 2000), pp. 143–59.

5 ——
See e.g. Linda Garcia, "The Architecture of Global Network-ing Technologies," in S. Sassen (ed.), *Global Networks, Linked Cities* (London and New York: Routledge, 2002).

by the hyper-mobility of some of its components/products/outcomes. Both capital fixity and mobility are located in a temporal frame where speed is ascendant and consequential. This type of capital fixity cannot be fully captured in a description of its material and locational features, i.e., in a topographical reading.

Conceptualizing digitization and globalization along these lines creates operational and rhetorical openings for recognizing the ongoing importance of the material world even in the case of some of the most de-materialized activities.

The spatialities of the center

Information technologies have not eliminated the importance of massive concentrations of material resources but have, rather, reconfigured the interaction of capital fixity and hyper-mobility. The complex management of this interaction has given some cities a new competitive advantage. The vast new economic topography that is being implemented through electronic space is one moment, one fragment, of an even vaster economic chain that is in good part embedded in non-electronic spaces. There is today no fully virtualized firm or economic sector. Even finance, the most digitized, de-materialized and globalized of all activities has a topography that weaves back and forth between actual and digital space. To different extents in different types of sectors and different types of firms, a firm's tasks now are distributed across these two kinds of spaces; further, the actual configurations are subject to considerable transformation as tasks are computerized or standardized, markets are further globalized, and so on. The combination of the new capabilities for mobility along with patterns of concentration and operational features of the cutting edge sectors of advanced economies suggests that spatial concentration remains as a key feature of these sectors. But it is not simply a continuation of older patterns of spatial concentration. Today there is no longer a simple straightforward relation between centrality and such geographic entities as the downtown, or the central business district. In the past, and up to quite recently in fact, centrality was synonymous with the downtown or the CBD. The new technologies and organizational forms have altered the spatial correlates of centrality.[6]

Given the differential impacts of the capabilities of the new information technologies on specific types of firms and of sectors of the economy, the spatial correlates of the "center" can assume several geographic forms, likely to be operating simultaneously at the macro level. Thus the center can be the CBD, as it still is largely for some of the leading sectors, notably finance, or an alternative form of CBD, such as Silicon Valley. Yet even as the CBD in major international business centers remains a strategic site for the leading industries, it is one profoundly reconfigured by technological and economic change.[7] Further, there are often sharp differences in the patterns assumed by this reconfiguring of the central city in different parts of the world.[8]

Second, the center can extend into a metropolitan area in the form of a grid of nodes of intense business activity. One might ask whether a spatial organization characterized by dense strategic nodes spread over a broader region does in fact constitute a new form of organizing the territory of the "center," rather than, as in the more conventional view, an instance of suburbanization or geographic dispersal. Insofar as these various nodes are articulated through digital networks, they represent a new geographic correlate of the most advanced type of "center." This is a partly de-territorialized space of centrality.[9]

Third, we are seeing the formation of a trans-territorial "center" constituted via intense economic transactions in the network of global cities. These transactions take place partly in digital space and partly through conventional transport and travel. The result is a multiplication of often highly specialized circuits connecting sets of cities.[10] These networks of major international business centers constitute new geographies of centrality. The most powerful of these new geographies of centrality at the global level binds the major international financial and business centers: New York, London, Tokyo, Paris, Frankfurt, Zurich, Amsterdam, Los Angeles, Sydney, Hong Kong, among others. But this geography now also includes cities such as Bangkok, Seoul, Taipei, Sao Paulo, Mexico City. In the case of a complex landscape such as Europe's we see in fact several geographies of centrality, one global, others continental and regional.

Fourth, new forms of centrality are being constituted in electronically generated spaces. For instance, strategic components of the financial

—— 7

Pablo Cicolella and Iliana Mignaqui, "The Spatial Reorganization of Buenos Aires," in Global Networks, Linked Cities; Susan S. Fainstein, The City Builders (Lawrence, Kansas: Kansas University Press, 2001); Sueli Ramos Schiffer, "Sao Paulo: Articulating a Cross-Border Regional Economy," in Global Networks, Linked Cities.

—— 9

This regional grid of nodes represents, in my analysis, a reconstitution of the concept of region. Further, it should not be confused with the suburbanization of economic activity. I conceive of it as a space of centrality partly located in older socio-economic geographies, such as that of the suburb or the larger metropolitan region, yet as distinct precisely because it is a space of centrality. Far from neutralizing geography the regional grid is likely to be embedded in conventional forms of communication infrastructure, notably rapid rail and highways connecting to airports. Ironically perhaps, conventional infrastructure is likely to maximize the economic benefits derived from telematics. I think this is an important issue that has been lost somewhat in discussions about the neutralization of geography through telematics. For an exception see Michel Péraldi and Evelyne Perrin (eds.), Reseaux productifs et territoires urbains (Toulouse: Presses Universitaires du Mirail, 1996).

—— 6

Several of the organizing hypotheses in the global city model concern the conditions for the continuity of centrality in advanced economic systems in the face of major new organizational forms and technologies that maximize the possibility for geographic dispersal. See new "Introduction" in the updated edition of The Global City (2001). For a variety of perspectives see, e.g., J. Landrieu, N. May, T. Spector and P. Veltz (eds.), La Ville éclatée (La Tour d'Aigues: Editiones de l'Aube, 1998); Ilan Salomon, "Telecommunications, Cities and Technological Opportunism," The Annals of Regional Science, vol. 30, no. 1 (1996), pp. 75–90.

—— 8

E.g. Peter Marcuse and Ronald van Kempen, Globalizing Cities: A New Spatial Order? (Oxford: Blackwell, 2000).

—— 10

E.g. Yue-Man Yeung, Globalization and Networked Societies (Honolulu: University of Hawai'i Press, 2000).

industry operate in such spaces. The relation between digital and actual space is complex and varies among different types of economic sectors.

What does contextuality mean in this setting?

These networked sub-economies operating partly in actual space and partly in globe-spanning digital space cannot easily be contextualized in terms of their surroundings. Nor can the individual firms and markets. The orientation of this type of sub-economy is simultaneously towards itself and towards the global. The intensity of internal transactions in such a sub-economy (whether global finance or cutting edge high-tech sectors) is such that it overrides all considerations of the broader locality or urban area within which it exists.

On another, larger scale, in my research on global cities I found rather clearly that these sub-economies develop a stronger orientation towards the global markets than to their hinterlands. Thereby they override a key proposition in the urban systems literature, to wit, that cities and urban systems integrate and articulate national territory. This may have been the case during the period when mass manufacturing and mass consumption were the dominant growth machines in developed economies and thrived on national economic processes. Today, the ascendance of digitized, globalized, de-materialized sectors such as finance, has diluted that articulation with the larger national economy and the immediate hinterland.

The articulation of these sub-economies with other zones and sectors in their immediate socio-spatial surroundings are of a special sort. There are the various highly priced services that cater to the workforce, from up-scale restaurants and hotels to luxury shops and cultural institutions, typically part of the socio-spatial order of these new sub-economies. But there are also various low-priced services that cater to the firms and to the households of the workers and which rarely "look" like they are part of the advanced corporate economy. The demand by firms and households for these services actually links two worlds that we think of as radically distinct. It is particularly a third instance that concerns me here, the large portions of the urban surrounding that have little connection to these world-market oriented sub-economies, even though physically proximate. It is these that engender a question about context and its meaning when it comes to these sub-economies.

What then is the "context," the local, here? The new networked sub-economy occupies a strategic geography, partly de-territorialized, that cuts across borders and connects a variety of points on the globe. It occupies only a fraction of its "local" setting, its boundaries are not those of the city where it is partly located, nor those of the "neighborhood." This sub-economy interfaces the intensity of the vast concentration of very material resources it needs when it hits the ground and the fact of its global span or cross-border geography. Its interlocutor is not the surrounding, the context, but the fact of the global.

I am not sure what this tearing away of the context and its replacement with the fact of the global could mean for urban practice and theory. The strategic operation is not the search for a connection with the "surroundings," the context. It is, rather, installation in a strategic cross-border geography constituted through multiple "locals." In the case of the economy I see a re-scaling: old hierarchies – local, regional, national, global – do not hold. Going

James Polshek and Richard Olcott: Sign, Symbol and the Presidential Library
Interview by Macky McCleary and Jennifer Silbert

Macky What we wanted to talk about today was the way in which architecture can change and exchange meaning, culturally, formally and politically. How to access sign and symbol, and how this library can or will affect the Clinton legacy. Can you first take us through the process and the basic architectural concepts of the building. How were you chosen as the architects?
James I've heard that the president considered almost a hundred architects.
Richard He had the Pritzker Prize that year at the White House, so there were a hundred of them right there. I know he interviewed several. I think some of them may have even done some sketching. We don't know why none of that went anywhere. But they went back to the beginning. At that point they asked a close friend of theirs, Cathy Hockersmith, the White House decorator,

and an old Little Rock friend, if she knew anybody. And thro various people she knows and we know, we were recomme to them. So, we sent a portfolio of our work to the White Ho which was favorably received…
James The chemistry, personal chemistry, is a major hidd factor when somebody is interviewing architects.
Richard Our first meeting with the president was really a informal discussion. We asked him how he envisioned the Library. One of the things that he laid out at the get-go, tha was to be inviting and grand, but very accessible, visually, intellectually, and otherwise. He did not want a black box a not want anything hermetic, forbidding or mausoleum-like
James Yes. He would say over and over, he likes modern a tecture: believes in the future, openness. So the issues of accessibility and emotional accessibility, information acces these were issues not only in the building, but in his presi as well. This was actually one of his Executive Orders that just turned around in the last couple of weeks or so.

to the next scale in terms of size is no longer how integration is achieved. The local now transacts directly with the global, the global installs itself in the local and the global is itself constituted through a multiplicity of local situations.

In conclusion

The meanings and roles of architecture and planning centered in older traditions of permanence are irrevocably destabilized in today's complex cities – that is, cities marked by digital networks, acceleration, massive infrastructures for connectivity, and growing estrangement. Those older meanings do not disappear, they remain important. But they cannot address comfortably these newer meanings.

There are, clearly, multiple ways of positing the challenges facing architecture and planning as practice and as theorization today. In emphasizing the crucial place of cities for architecture, I construct a problematic that is not only positioned but also, perhaps inevitably, partial. It is different from that of neo-traditionalist architects who are also concerned about the current urban condition. And it is different from a problematic focused on how current conditions are changing the profession and its opportunities, or, if critical, one which centers its critical stance in questions of the growing distance between the winners and the losers in the profession.

Architecture and planning, further, need to confront the massiveness of the urban experience, the overwhelming presence of massive architectures and massive infrastructures in today's cities, and the overwhelming logic of utility that organizes much of the investments in cities. At the same time, these cities are full of underused spaces, often characterized more by past, gone, meanings than current meaning. These spaces are part of the interiority of a city yet lie outside its organizing utility-driven logics and spatial frames. This opens up a critical problematic about the current urban condition in ways that take it beyond the notions of high-tech architecture, virtual spaces, simulacra, theme parks. All of the latter are too easy.

This calls for urbanists able to navigates multiple forms of knowledge and introduce the possibility of an architectural practice located in spaces – such as intersections of multiple transport and communication networks – where the naked eye or the engineer's imagination sees no shape, no possibility of a form, pure infrastructure and utility. Further, how do we detect the possible architectures of spaces that are construed as empty silences, non-existences, for architectural practices centered in permanence.

d He also made it very clear that he was underwhelmed ◆ other presidential libraries. And they are wildly different. st ones are the ones that he admires the most, Kennedy's, and Carter's.

er The Democrats.

d Most of the Carter Library is actually not the library. is a whole policy think tank, outreach organization, Habitat manity and all that stuff that is there, and that comprises rds of the building; the library is sort of over here. And Carter, as everyone knows, been more effective ex- ent than president.

We asked him, what's your favorite building in Washington? d the East Building. We said, good answer. Then he spent a ime talking about Thomas Jefferson's architecture and its n to his politics. Certainly agreed with him on that. He bout, but had not been to the Rose Planetarium, and he about Gehry's building in Bilbao, what we thought it would ke in 50 years. It was a good question.

The William J. Clinton Presidential Center, Little Rock, Arkansas
Architects: Polshek Partnership
Photography: Timothy Hursley

2ND PLACE: DESIGN COMPETITIONS

Dz0 Architects

Competition
L'Arca/Auchan Competition, 2001

Site/location
Retail facility to be built in different places in different scales

Atelier Bow Wow

Competition
Housing plan

Site/location
Suburban area near Tokyo, Japan

Florian Haydn & Partners

Competition
Masterplan

Site/location
Cable Factory-KDAG, Vienna, Austria

**Servo
(David Erdman, Marcelyn Gow, Ulrika Karlsson, Chris Perry)**

Competition
Lobbi_ports 2002

Site/location
Speculative hotel proposal commissioned by the Smithsonian National Design Museum for the "New Hotels for Global Nomads"

In collaboration with
Chris Kabatsi, Mike Mangelli, Tyen Masten, Clare Olsen (design team)

**Kinetic Design Group
(Michael Fox, Axel Kilian, Jeffery Tsui, Juintow Lin)**

Competition
Domus/BBJ Design Competition

Site/location
Boeing Business Jet interior

Tim Durfee

Competition
SCI-Arc expansion

Site/location
Los Angeles, California

Naga Studio Architecture

Competition
The Grand Egyptian Museum (GEM)

Site/location
The Pyramids Plateau, Giza, Egypt

In design competitions, 2nd place has historically been the realm of the radical idea, thoughtfully conceived, but for some reason trapped in "concept" rather than lending itself to realization. Timid juries and tight budgets have propagated this trend throughout the years, and in this section we have chosen non-winning entries from several recent competitions and hope to shed light on some of the brilliance that goes largely unnoticed.

Jennifer So where did you begin with the library?

Richard Have you ever been to Little Rock? Little Rock is where the Mississippi meets the mountains. It was once upon a time a river town, and then a railroad town. And then it turned it's back on the river and it's a kind of a forgotten place.

James Our site is right downtown, next to a major interstate, and a short walk from the central downtown, which makes it unique among presidential libraries, because most are quite inaccessible. I think Clinton was offered lots of other sites that were easy to build on, but further away. This one is a real brown field, a bunch of abandoned warehouses, and requires a lot of cleanup work. He was very interested in it being a downtown catalyst.

Richard Yes, that's pretty fundamental. The site is 28 acres, right in the downtown, which is a pretty significant urban park. There will be easily a million people a year there. There are little old ladies who will want to see the Oval Office, and school children who want to learn something they never learned before. And incredibly intelligent scholars who will be digging really deep.

You have got to satisfy all of those people.

James The red building is a beautiful 1899 train station. There is also a beautiful railroad bridge leading directly into the middle of the site. When we saw the site for the first time it was very cold, if you recall, when we walked up on top of the train station. We saw that bridge and both of us said, that has to stay. It has to be part of the scheme. It fit so perfectly into the president's rhetoric: the bridge to the 21st century. This was our napkin sketch. We met in the Map Room of the White House. He wasn't there on time which was odd because in general he was quite punctual, and paid undivided attention. No aides or anything like that. This night he was late. When he came in, he was very flushed and red, glassy-eyed and agitated, and he said, "As we speak they are killing our children." It was 6 o'clock on the night of the Colombine massacre. But he gave us 45 undisturbed minutes to look at this document; and, he really focused on it.

Richard At one point he said, "We should move along, because I have this Kosovo thing I have to deal with." He was amazing. He

has the ability to focus on something, and everything else f away.

Macky How did that first meeting change the way you saw project?

Richard We went back and thought about this a little more. Jim mentioned, we went up on top of the building and thoug hmm, maybe it shouldn't face the river. If you look across th river, all you see is the other side of the river; whereas, if yo look up the river, you see this wonderful perspective of wha known as the six bridges.

James There are two aspects; that's the first: the six bridge other one is enhancing Little Rock's park system. We did th previous schemes for him, but all of the schemes that were parallel to the river ended up covering a great deal of the p The minute you turn it perpendicular to the river and elevat like a bridge fragment, the site is preserved and the park ru continuously underneath it.

Richard The whole idea of the connecting bridge became

Dz0 Architects

Blurred Landscape

To talk about the porosity of a shopping mall's envelope is to put a fresh spin on a traditionally self-contained type of brief and to think in terms of active integration, of taking the building out into its context. Via an open-ended structure the project offers a gradual shift from the urban to landscape, from motorway to greenery. By turning its back to the main access road it defines its own site as a transitional zone in which the sales area, the car park and the landscape all contribute to actively breaking-down accepted boundaries. The sales area does not come across as controlled and methodically laid out, having been conceived, on the contrary, as differentiated: specific yet fluid zones take shape around promotional, cultural and other events and are marked out by their own light, heat and sound characteristics. These zones determine the shape of the envelope, a sensitive film that registers and expresses the variety of the spaces inside it.

The shell, then, filters and regulates, functioning as a surface for interchange with the exterior and containing such necessary facilities as ventilation and smoke evacuation equipment. The new shopping center is not a function of its look or brand image; rather, the concept is integration-based and operates differently according to specific needs. While it is true that the shell has a descriptive function, this is above all because the richness of its "texture" is expressive of the variety of its smoothly differentiated internal spaces. This shopping center becomes a distinctive part of the landscape because it deliberately blurs its identity, mingling the shrewd grid of its shell with vegetal textures as it implements gradations of layout and organization at floor level. Hence it combines efficiency and flexibility with an ecological, landscape-based approach to its own integration.

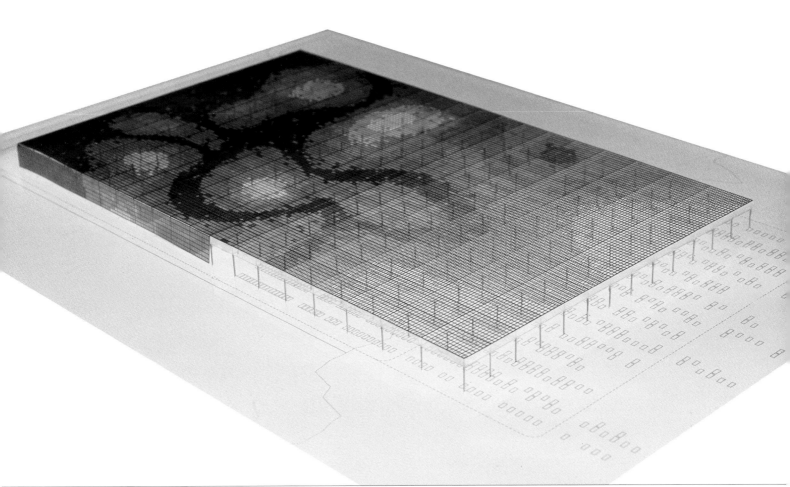

here. The railroad bridge and the building begin to enter dialogue with each other.

It's a diagram.

It's a napkin sketch.

on a White House men's room towel.

And he, of course, immediately seized onto the notion of bridge to the 21st century as an obvious metaphor for him. there is a dialogue with the bridge and train station, will be renovated to house the Clinton foundation and for Public Policy. There is a poignant overlay of past and there.

Well, the idea of restoring the river edge, we are doing a of things, restoring it to its ancient ecological past to t, and then to the west, you will see those vectors go out river, to create these pools, for an urban fishing ground. me more recreational as it reaches to the west toward

And as we mentioned, it is actually an extension of a

whole riverfront park system that the City of Little Rock has been working on for years.

James This was a critical moment. He really saw things. He had some real questions about the structure. There is a stair that comes dripping out of the building independent of its final support. He didn't like that. He immediately thought fire escape, which of course is what it is. So, it is now integrated into the structure.

Richard He is actually amazingly visually acute and articulate. Most impressive performance. He does not mince words when he feels he does not like something.

James It comes with the job.

Macky What is the specific connection between the personality of the president and its manifestation in the library. It seems like he is exerting an enormous amount of force here as a personality.

James In a larger sense, we joke about it. In a way it's true. Reagan's library is very ranch-house-cowboy like; Lyndon Johnson's imperial Gordon Bunshaft building, which has kind of

a knockoff of the Beinecke library. Gerald Ford's is completely blank, totally, absolutely. Carter's is landscaping, beautifully landscaped. So, in a relative sense, this is a very highly intellectualized scheme and it was very consciously arrived at. It is the most intellectual of all the libraries.

Richard Library is sort of a misnomer.

James It shouldn't be called that.

Richard They are half museum and half archive.

Macky In studying the website, I started to understand the fact that Clinton being called the internet president was having a big effect on his understanding of this archive. Are the computer archives part of the museum or part of other archives?

Richard The Clinton Library will be much more interactive and is much more based upon media and software and stuff, and much less upon physical objects and traditional museum pieces. The space itself is configured as a library. The example used is the great library at Trinity College Dublin, which is a double height space.

Atelier Bow Wow   **Living Field**

The project is 1 hour from Tokyo by newly completed rail line. The theme of competition is a new life style for the region. Our intent is to discover the specific house type of this area, a typology that lies between the suburban house and weekend house type.

The site inclines to the pond at the south and is bordered by a main road at the north. Eleven north-south connector streets divide the area into twelve

blocks – a simple street pattern that maximizes the private property in this residential area. Each property has one long east-west house with a surrounding garden. The gardens provide public spaces such as farmland, flower farm, pool, café, parking, 3 on 3, fishing pond, skateboard park, open air gallery, etc. The houses are private, transcending to public gardens. The area becomes a tissue of sequential fields characterized by different activities, in order to produce and sustain the lifestyle between suburban and provincial.

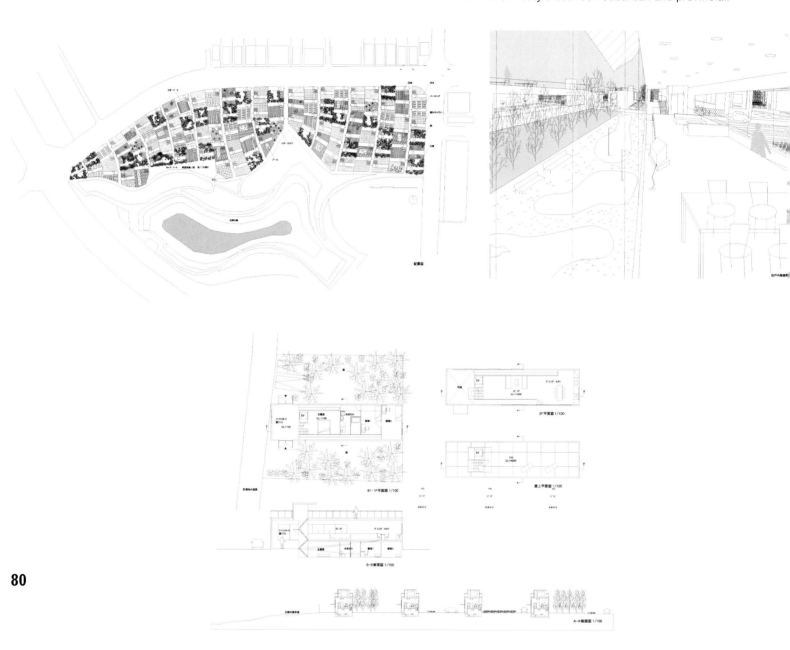

80

James Which Clinton has visited many times.
Richard In the first museum level you come in the lobby and go up an escalator. You go first through an oval orientation room. And then you go to the left. There is the big table in the Cabinet Room, that is where they lay out the sort of themes of the Clinton presidency in front of every one of the different cabinet members. And then the big Trinity College space is to the left of that, which has these alcoves. Each alcove is a theme: One is gun control, one is Africa, one is Christmas at the White House; there are all kinds of different themes, but most of these on this floor are all policy initiatives.
Macky You talked about how different the Clinton Library was from the other ones, by your design and by his design. Is it necessary for him to have this bridge into the future, this separation from both the history of existing presidential libraries, and the things that he does not want to be remembered about his own history?
Richard I think that they have addressed that head on. For

example, there is an alcove in there to deal with impeachment.
James You can't ignore that.
Richard They know that. But that is part of his belief. That it is all there, and that it is all glass and it is all accessible and you can look at it.
James This ideology, this transparency and the free dissemination of information, is manifest in the architecture…
Richard That is the basic tenet of the whole enterprise, absolutely. But, you know these things are complicated. For instance, in the JFK Library, for many years, there was no mention of assassination because the family didn't want to talk about it – for obvious reasons.
James For Reagan there was no mention of Iran-Contra until recently. And in Johnson's, Lady Bird kept Viet Nam down to little mentions.
Richard But you think about presidencies where more has happened. You know, only FDR can top. You had World War II, civil rights, Viet Nam, and it is all jammed into this tiny little exhibition.

And then there's this huge space that has nothing. That is ▮ architectural volume supposed to be awe-inspiring. It is er▮ the Clinton library, they are very conscious of it being ope▮ accessible. History belongs to the victors and they get to w▮ their way, just like everybody else has, but it is certainly th▮ intention to put it all in there.
James The intention is to dignify, no question about it. But ▮ had to struggle with it on the inside. It is a little frustrating ▮ only the architect, not get into the exhibit too, which is the ▮ substance of it.
Richard They have a whole other set of meetings we are r▮ part of. They are all sitting around, pushing around ideas, ▮ disagreeing about how something should be presented, ho▮ much emphasis. They really care, for obvious reasons.
Jennifer Can you tell us a little bit about what you think th▮ building is going to mean to the visitors, and what it might ▮ to the president, and what it actually means to you two as t▮ architects.

Florian Haydn   Urban Tattoo
Florian Haydn & Partners

The basis of the project is a growth-orientated strategy for differentiated urban structures. The point of departure is a basic codex for the site arranged as individual elements for development, atmosphere and thought processes. These form the seeds for growth processes and condition the site for prospective participating architects, who read this codex as a pre-existing landscape and have to react to it. In the development codex, the term "infrastructure" is to be redefined. The seeds for the infrastructure are articulated according to the degree to which they are public, and divided into process-oriented initiatives. The urban structure is no longer drawn from urban spatial considerations, but from the multifaceted over-lapping of the preconditions and activities and their interrelationships.

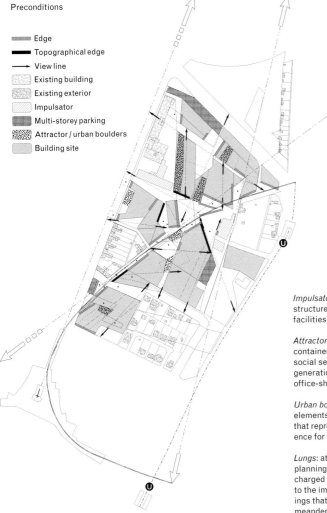

Preconditions

- ▨ Edge
- ▬ Topographical edge
- → View line
- ▦ Existing building
- ▦ Existing exterior
- ▨ Impulsator
- ▦ Multi-storey parking
- ▨ Attractor / urban boulders
- ▨ Building site

Impulsators: very public infra-structure-seeds – e.g., for culture facilities

Attractors: expandable social containers (for initiative groups, social self-organization, mixed-generation accommodation, office-sharing etc.)

Urban boulders: individual elements of the infrastructure that represent points of reference for the structure

Lungs: atmospheric codes; the planning blueprint of a tension-charged landscape comparable to the image of rural surroundings that is given by the meandering of a river or the rises of a chain of hills along which a city develops

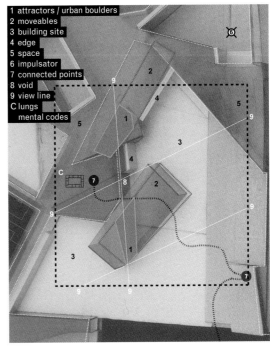

1 attractors / urban boulders
2 moveables
3 building site
4 edge
5 space
6 impulsator
7 connected points
8 void
9 view line
C lungs
mental codes

Preconditions detail

Well, you have to see it in the context of lots of buildings in the context of the culture of this office and its attitude making architecture. Now, when you see it in that way, each projects, whether it be Stanford, Smith College, Williams, which are all academic institutions, or scientific, or mental or cultural institutions, they all have identities. ave a sense of themselves.

er This building in particular is shifting in its identity, in nse that it is a library, but it's a presidential library. It is a ort of typology we're talking about. Referring to the library, o a museum, it's also a shrine, and it is a mausoleum. It has relationship to power.

Absolutely.

rd I think that we definitely set out to try and break that at the specific direction of the president. At our very first ng with the president, he said right off the bat, "I hate these s, I don't like any of these and I don't want to use them." er Because you are also in a position where you are

creating a new mold, without a firm precedent.

James The personality of the person, but beyond that, the kind of basic theory behind a building like this, which has to represent humane values in ways which are fairly obvious.

Richard It was FDR's idea. Before that, you took your papers home. FDR said, this belongs to the people of the United States, not to him. And that was the whole idea, it was openness from the beginning. The way it works is as a government building. It will be run by the National Archives and Records Administration. Privately funded. We build it. We give them the keys. They run it. And it can only be X square feet. There is a whole congressional mandate with guidelines. It has to be this big, and no bigger, because they do not want anybody to have too much fun in their presidential library.

James There is no precedent. We can show you the other libraries, they are not precedents for this.

Richard The museum also has to entertain; so, there may also be some pure entertainment.

Macky The idea behind this library, of re-creating the idea of the presidential library is a way of re-creating the idea of the presidency, or trying to have an effect on the view of the presidency, even while there is a current sitting president who is constantly in opposition to whatever those ideas would be.

Richard He believes very much, and will put his money where his mouth is. The building will be open, like all of the laws he signed. It will be environmentally responsible. It is an opportunity.

Jennifer One that has to do directly with the presentation of a legacy.

Macky We talked about how Clinton was obviously a huge part of the entire process, the president himself, in terms of the design. How has working with him affected your opinion of him as a president and as a person?

James I think we both should give our own answers because they may be a little different, but I don't think very much so.

Richard I was always a great fan. But being close to him and actually seeing this kind of photographic memory, his ability to

Servo

David Erdman
Marcelyn Gow
Ulrika Karlsson
Chris Perry

Lobbi-ports is a speculative project which sees the future of hotel lobbies as cultural terminals or ports of entry for cities. Constructing an "implanted" curtain wall which carries both people and soft infrastructure, the system re-wires and re-distributes the circuits of existing towers bought for new hotels. Proposing that hotel lobbies will become the urban living room for local urban dwellers as well as serve the function of cultural destination for the tourist, the Lobbi-port will thus allow for stays which extend beyond a meal, check in, or a drink and open the possibility for new modes of interactivity and atmosphere to emerge, where the hotel TV is the lobby and the

lounge has become the room. By occupying the wall lobbies are situated vertically (up from the ground floor) constructing an urban condition which drifts from the street and the ground up into the hotel tower. The newly implanted enclosure system is conceptualized as a physical software to supply these spaces with light sound, and video. Using programmable LED sheets, video streams through the curtain wall at various speeds, drifting, cascading, creating visual and informational eddies. The video impresses the flow, distribution and direction of information through the implants while simultaneously re-distributing the cultural and pedestrian urbanism of the tower.

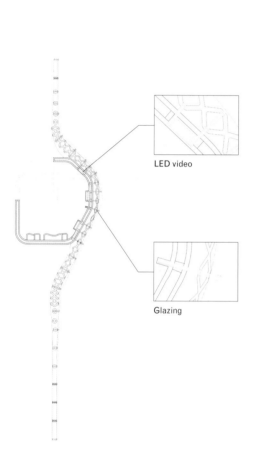

LED video

Glazing

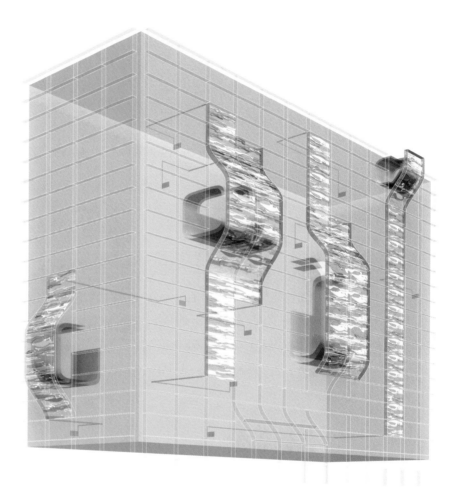

focus, was really very impressive. He is extremely presidential; that was the great surprise. You know, I was kind of amazed at that, because he is a big guy, physically impressive, but intellectually, you just, you know you're with a gem. Plus, he is very approachable, and he looks you in the eye, he doesn't look over your shoulder.

James It is actually amazing to see other people around him. He is the most personally magnetic person. That is why he is who he is. He is affectionate and he's very warm.

Richard But, as I said before, he does not mince words when he does not like something. I think he's just a good ole boy from Arkansas, full of anecdotes and a southern accent, combined with this super poly-math intellectual; he is just an amazing combination of things. He was on Letterman just before Christmas. 10 minutes, the most cogent world-view, the exact opposite of everything that is going on. Boom! The most articulate performance you can possibly imagine. Right in the middle Dave interrupts and says, you know, I think maybe you still are the president.

Jennifer This is from the Washington Post, and it says: It is here on the banks of the Arkansas River that Clinton and his adherents will wage their argument through the decades," and that has to do with what you are physically building there, in my opinion. And allowing President Clinton to create his own legacy. Do you feel that is happening with the construction of the library?

James Well, he is not manipulating his own legacy. I think he is gathering the documents together and the narratives that will tell people what the legacy is and they will have to make certain judgments. But, when you think about the examples that we used, of Iran Contra and Viet Nam and the assassination, which is not in the same league, of course, but the fact is, the kind of gravity of those events, compared to the gravity of Clinton's problems, make Clinton's problems really rather minor, in my view.

Richard When you go there and you have absorbed the totality of all of those alcoves, you will realize that there are so many different initiatives that they were doing at the same time, and all add up to something bigger; that's what they want to get.

James You have a better sense of the complexity of the presidency.

Macky Interdependency.

Richard And, if anything, they have been accused of havin big an agenda, and not being able to get one thing done, because they were trying to get everything done.

Jennifer We are running out of tape. Do you have any last remarks to sum up your experiences working with the pres on the presidential library?

James Build it, and they will come. [laughter] It has been v very thrilling. And actually, it is not over, but it has had an e on the whole office. It kind of reinforced old traditions and allowed people to explore new ideas and their own ideas ir service of something that is much larger, that is the most important aspect of it. We do not deal with signatures neces though they are there.

Macky There is a difference between a signature and a language. It's the Thomas Jefferson thing.

Kinetic Design Group

Michael Fox
Axel Kilian
Jeffery Tsui
Juintow Lin

The motivation for this project lies in creating interior design solutions that are flexible and adaptive, and at instances, responsive and intelligently active with respect to the changing individual, social and climatic contexts. Accordingly, the goal was to provide a responsive interior space that can be configured as prescribed by the users prior to a specific flight as well as partially reconfigured in-flight.

The design proposal introduces to the interior three basic kinetic components, namely sectors, which display variable location (mobility) and variable geometry (transformability). The sectors can technically operate independently; as a complete system, they divide and define zones of the program in the interior. Each is equipped with/provides the technical and the physical/spatial apparatus necessary for various parts of the program.

A building designed like the body would have a system of bones and muscles and a brain than can tell it how to adapt. It would combine the kinetic potential of mobility and transformation with the embedded computation of sensing and response.

Reconfigurable elements: elements pass each other

We did have this conversation once. We wouldn't do this president. If there is one president who I would choose to brary, it would definitely be this one.

There is a magnetism that seems to infect everything. Everyone that has come within one degree of separation. You know what it is more than anything else? It demonthat this president cared; because almost all — I do not say all of the presidential libraries, but the case, for e, of Kennedy, this had an awful lot to do with Jackie and e of style. She was very involved in the selection of the ct. But in Bush 41, it was just like corporate business as here was HOK. And for many, many of the libraries, that way it was. Roosevelt's, of course, was quite different e that was the homestead and there was a hint of aristoc-the Hudson River Valley.

The last American king.

But this guy really cared.

Tim Durfee

An Urban Attractor

SCI-Arc is a place for the exploration and contemplation of space, form, and the built environment. It is also a place for caffeinated debate, reckless experimentation, and occasional end-of-the-week unwinding with the assistance of half-chilled domestic beer. This proposal introduces new spaces that are both specifically conducive to these important activities and flexible to other uses, appropriations, and improvisations.

As a relentlessly linear structure, the building provokes continual awareness of one's position along a closed path. As a reaction to this, this project attempts to recover for building's occupants a sense of frameless continuity by allowing the physical and perceptual flow of people to the roof –

visually out to the city and countryside and, aspirationally, beyond. The quality of frameless-ness is also evoked in the use of rhythmic systems – specifically the systems of torqued louvers, staggered struts, and waffle-walls – which resist singularity and objecthood, while producing effects that vary with different speeds and proximities of encounter.

Heat gain/light: SCI-Arc's building is an extraordinary asset as a landmark and symbol of the school's independent spirit. It is also long. So long that the surface area itself – specifically its exposure to direct sun nearly year-round – can be understood as a uniquely valuable commodity. The design emerges from responses to the existing building that are both conceptual and practical.

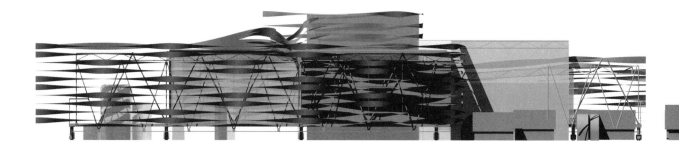

Tarek Naga
Naga Studio Architecture

Osiris Re-Membered

Nuk pu kheper em khepera.......
kheper-na .....kheper kheperu......
kheper kheperu .....neb em -khet kheper-a asht
kheperu em per em re-a

I am he who came into becoming,
becoming what I created
The creator of the creations...
having created my own becoming,
I created multitudes
That came forth from my logos, Ra [...............]
came forth into day

From the Papyrus of Anni of "Coming Forth into Day,"
The Egyptian Book of the Dead

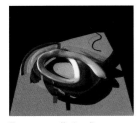

Temporary galleries: (incompossibility membrane)

Gallery section diagrams

Osiris: In the creation mythology of Ancient Egypt, Osiris is pre-imminent as the quintessential symbol of resurrection and regeneration of life forms; the becoming.

Not unlike the resurrected Osiris, Egyptian artifacts, royal mummies, temples and tombs, were blundered, mutilated and their "limbs" scattered all over the world. GEM becomes the act of their re-memberment and re-memberance.

Membranes of re-memberment and re-membrance: Multiple layers of esoteric hidden mysteries create three distinct spatial flows: a *flow of potentiality* (a cybernetic emanation; the virtual museum layer), a *flow of virtuality* (the temporary exhibitions layer) and a *flow of incompossibility* (the collective of all the Osireses of the Royal mummies). The esoteric inner flows are encircled by the exoteric, manifest world of the permanent collection artifacts that engenders a milieu encompassing Ancient Egypt's meta-geography, its cosmology, the precepts of its netters, and the after-world.

Egypt re-membered: Osiris re-membered, operates on multiple levels of complexities emanating from the essence of the "mind" of Ancient Egypt. As for modern Egypt, that principle stands as a painful reminder of the legacy of her ancient heritage having been mutilated and dismembered throughout history.

Egyptology will be coming home. Egypt's long history will, at last, be re-membered.

Entire scheme

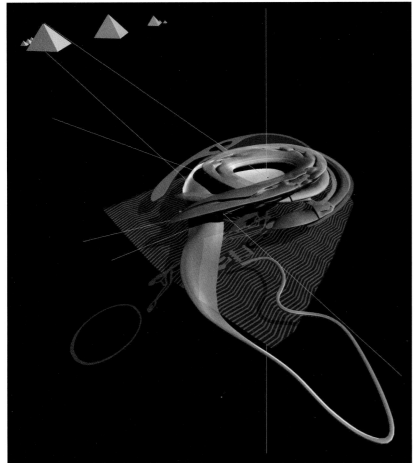

Scheme diagrams

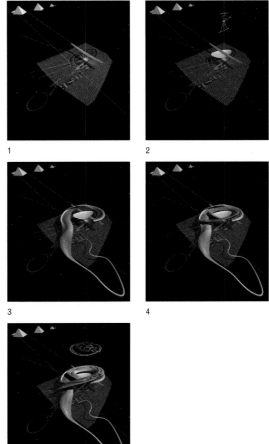

THE ASIAN ARCADES PROJECT: PROGRESSIVE POROSITY

LESLIE LU

Porosity

Walter Benjamin, in his 1925 essay entitled "Naples,"[1] explored the idea of vitality and variety in the modern city. Benjamin cited his observations of the urban, social, spatial and temporal organization of Naples in distinction to Georg Lukacs's pessimistic view of the homogeneity of future cities – the sameness of urban experience, urban life and urban form, as a result of the predetermination of collective consciousness by the conditions of the market economy in a modern capitalist society.[2] Benjamin would later explore and develop this notion in a series of essays collected as *The Arcades Project*.[3]

Benjamin was fascinated by Naples' urban space, a condition he called spatial porosity, meaning in one instance the permeation of privacy by communal life, and in another, the interpenetration of day and night, street and home. To Benjamin, porosity was a bridge between action and architecture. It highlighted the improvised character of everyday life as dramatic performance.[4] Benjamin also hinted at the confluence of public life and private rituals in Naples as a possible situation in which modern city life can coexist with local sub-cultures.

In post-colonial Asian cities like Hong Kong similar conditions of urban porosity exist. Hong Kong's urban environment is devoid of the cultural conditions that mark the traditional "world cities" of the West. There are no memorable public spaces, no refined residential fabric, and no exemplary monuments to religion, politics, art, knowledge or culture.

Porosity, then can be interpreted as a lack of clear spatial divisions and boundaries between urban phenomena. In a high-density city like Hong Kong where open spaces are at a minimum, hidden areas of hyper-porosity are covert foci, centering fresh, strange organizational systems.

Hong Kong's growth followed a master plan of concentrated development on reclaimed land. Reclamation has long been employed as the method of choice to create land, to keep in pace with the rapid urban expansion of the central business districts on both sides of Victoria Harbour. Concentric layers of "new earth" were created along the coastline, structured by hierarchical patterns of traffic infrastructure creating isolated islands/strips and unrelated plots earmarked for development (fig. 1). This infrastructure-driven development strategy, coupled with strict adherence to zoning laws and building codes, resulted in hyper-density; an engine tuned for the production and consumption of wealth (fig. 2).

In the case of Hong Kong Island, with its hilly terrain and tiered ring-road system, the east-west boundaries between districts are more elastic than the north-south edges (fig. 3). Only two major north-south traffic arteries exist in the Central District of Hong Kong, both of which are high-speed connectors. The up-hill escalator system is the only north-south pedestrian traffic infrastructure of any significance.

The complex urban form of Hong Kong is further structured by three formal systems – the "first form" is the legacy of a maturing real estate-driven economy – small plot ownership

1 ———
Walter Benjamin, *Reflections: Essays, Aphorisms, Autobiographical Writings*, trans. Edmund Jephcott (New York: Harcourt, 1979), p. 163.

2 ———
Georg Lukacs, *History and Class Consciousness: Studies in Marxist Dialectics*, trans. Rodney Livingstone (London: Merlin Press, 1971).

3 ———
Walter Benjamin, *The Arcades Project*, trans. Howard Eiland & Kevin McLaughlin (Cambridge, Mass.: Belknap Press, 1999).

4 ———
Graeme Gilloch, *Myth and Metropolis: Walter Benjamin and the City* (Cambridge: Polity, 1996).

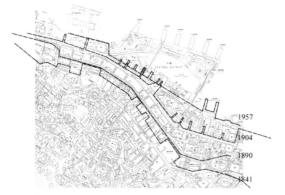

Fig. 1

Fig. 2

86

C. J. Kang
The Manhattan Project
2003
Oil on canvas

Fig. 3

Fig. 4

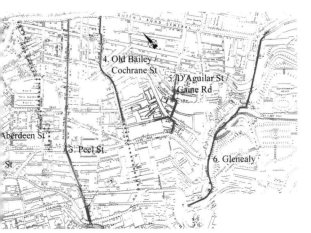

Fig. 5

The Central District Elevated Walkway System
The walkway network in the Central District began development as a joint venture between the Government and private developers, in an effort to connect the then largest reclamation site for the Hong Kong Stock Exchange (the Exchange Square) with the older central business district. Designed initially as a single elevated pedestrian walkway over a high speed artery (Connaught Road), the gesture became the system. The momentum for development began when the developers discovered that they were able to lease retail properties, at strategic destinations along the walkways, at the same or even twice the market rate as the street level stores.

In economic and political terms, the new elevated grounds are literally paved with gold, overturning any zoning or financial considerations for location. Connection and construction of such systems, a rare instance where capitalistic goals coincide with new urban design directions of Hong Kong. The result is a network of north-south oriented pedestrian walkways floating on top of the east-west vehicular spines, demonstrating an effective way to deal with one of the many conflicts of density in a contemporary mega-polis.

coupled with maximized development and height restrictions based solely on floor area ratio. The result is a seemingly random distribution of tightly packed pencil-thin towers of varying height on a rationally planned grid. A condition often described as chaotic, due to the lack of three dimensional regularity, order or refinement in the built fabric.

The "second form" emerged from vertical mixed-used zoning policy, resulting in a vertical mixture of programs and events, signified by illegal structures, wild greenery, and loud signage announcing function. In this "second form," a combination of savagery and anarchy reflects the beauty and confusion of the contemporary city, its improvisation and perpetual motion, independent of the urban plan.

The "third form" is a recent phenomenon emerging from pragmatic solutions to problems resulting from hyper-density. It attempts to facilitate pedestrian flow, to separate pedestrian and vehicular traffic, and to provide vital pedestrian links between new development and existing fabric. A new infrastructure system, conceived as simple elevated bridges and walkways, has over time evolved into a distinct and separate pedestrian network, linking existing landmarks and creating new urban foci. Although this development signaled the virtual abandonment of the street, the network of elevated walkways created a new urban configuration of Hong Kong: it became the "new ground" of the city, reorganizing flow with new connections, indifferent to existing urban patterns (figs. 4, 5). The idea of the "street in the air" as an urban datum is not new. However, the level of success experienced by Hong Kong is exceptional.

The growth and development of the elevated walkway network began in the late 1970s, concentrating primarily in the central business district and suburban satellite developments. The walkway has in current practice been adopted as a "quick fix remedy" for resolving circulation problems. Often treated as a formal expression in building design, the potential of this "new ground" was not explored in theory nor in practice until the unintended success of the up-hill escalator projects in revitalizing the SoHo district in the 1990s.

The up-hill escalator system

The up-hill escalator system completed in October of 1993 was conceived as a traffic reduction device offering a direct pedestrian link between the affluent mid-levels district and the elevated walkway network in the Central Business District. This north-south pedestrian link would potentially reduce the multi-tiered east-west vehicular traffic circumscribing the outlines of the island. By 1999 the escalator system had transformed the adjoining residential neighborhood into the most vital mixed-use district in Hong Kong. The recent development of the International Financial Centre (IFC) mega-complex and the water front traffic exchange initiated a new pedestrian link between the elevated walkways, the escalator, the new waterfront traffic network and the newest financial/stock exchange center.

Urban life in Hong Kong is traditionally linear in form. The roles of parks, piazzas and gardens in Hong Kong take on functions that change with the time of the day. They are by nature multipurpose spaces, festival grounds, concert sites, and improvised sports arenas. While these open spaces are fully utilized in key times, they lack any identity and are usually barren and lifeless when not in use.

A large number of western cities in pursuit of tourism have "treated" significant portions of their old street fabric with arcades, walking streets and/or special districts. Rarely does the insertion of mechanical infrastructure play any significant role in the pedestrian strategy. However, the walkways and mechanical people mover systems in Hong Kong have succeeded in expanding Benjamin's "spatial porosity" into the temporal dimension.

The porosity of space

The elevated network of walkways in Central, unhindered by conflicts with vehicular traffic, creates an autonomous condition that allows growth in any direction without regard for geographical conditions, city forms or street patterns.

Spatially, the network collides into the atriums of existing shopping centers, into the lobbies of office buildings. The network, a labyrinth in the city, allows a continuous motion from exterior into interior, rendering boundaries porous and space fuzzy, agitated and in constant motion.

The Sheung Wan District, the earliest urban settlement on Hong Kong Island, was once the primary residential district for Chinese workers working for foreign corporations in the Central District. It is a neighborhood of densely packed tenements with a distinctly mixed cultural character. The area currently renamed SoHo is an old residential enclave within Sheung Wan, a working class neighborhood where the street market still functions as the center of activities. This district has for decades resisted major commercial development, retaining its granular neighborhood fabric, texture and atmosphere. Unfortunately the low living standards have gradually led to the exodus of the young and the affluent (fig. 6).

The street life along the five narrow uphill streets, prior to the construction of the walkways, very much resembled Benjamin's streets of Naples in that they shared a certain cultural informality arising from poverty and a literal porosity arising from neglect and disrepair (fig. 7).

The porosity of time

The uphill escalator system differs from the Central walkway system in two significant ways. In addition to the merging of urban spaces, the escalator is completely exterior, meandering through the fabric, dividing and connecting. While most of the system is elevated on columns centered over the streets, the escalator makes a number of grade level landings and transfers on street-crossings, intersecting the east-west roadways and allowing travelers to board and disembark.

Fig. 6   Fig. 7

Undeniably, the volume of traffic generated by tourists and locals attracted by the convenient and unique travelling experience, the nostalgic charm of an older neighborhood untarnished by time, contributed significantly to the regeneration and subsequent transformation of SoHo.

Porosity here is signified by overlap of rate – the slow states of repose and contemplation; the speeding machines; the gait of pedestrians traveling up and down hill together with the mechanical rhythm of the infrastructure – the porosity of time. The gradual momentum of the escalator allows hidden sites and back alleys to be revealed, new shop frontage in the air assembled, new meanings and new character unveiled, a new and stranger space created.

The Asian Arcades Project: SoHo Escalator

The SoHo Escalator Project, a proposal to locate new escalator lines in SoHo, is an attempt to expand the interpretation of porosity. Despite its success, or perhaps because of it, the escalator system poses a challenge to the street. Given the existing urban form of SoHo (long rectangular blocks defined by north-south running streets separated by parallel service alleys and service courts), opportunities for east-west through block travel are limited.

A condition often overlooked in the urban development of Hong Kong but evident in the urban fabric of SoHo, is the north-south mid-block network of service alleys and service courts and the east-west running mid-block alleys connecting the uphill streets. The service courts themselves are lot-size terraces, relatively flat, most of them punctured with street connecting service lanes. In addition, a number of empty lots, too small or too isolated for building development, exist in different locations, forming a void-ridden fabric – a diagram of porous density.

However, the potential for an additional layer of porosity exists. The back alley network in SoHo taken as a whole resembles a root-like system.

The design process involves:
1 Analysis of the existing escalator line, locating major points of distinctive character and activities. Identifying potential vector flow of people in site-specific locations as directions suitable for extensions, and the mapping of urban voids within a 2–3 block vicinity,

identifying a condition 2 blocks east of the existing line as optimum location for infiltration.

2 Identification of buildings in varying degree of decay suited for transformation or demolition as references for potential program development.

3 Establishing a new escalator and walkway line connecting these voids.

4 Devising new "landings" with specific programs in these void spaces, implement these into points of attractions or simple interchanges, establishing a system of gathering and dispersal of flow.

5 Identifying site opportunities for interaction in the area between the two lines based on the criteria established in the urban mapping.

6 Establish a field of linkages and folds between the two lines based on proximity, the trajectory infiltration/flow of the people and by points of attractions based on thematic program of use.

7 Activate the urban blocks from the center, establishing two simultaneous direction of flow towards the edge (streets) and upwards. Creating a three dimensional "double loaded" condition bringing higher effectiveness and diminished adversity to the city streets, allowing a controlled mixture of vehicular traffic and pedestrianization in selected or alternate streets locations to happen.

8 Establishing thematic program of use, in line with the government's strategy to enhance and develop Hong Kong's future industries, in the financial services sector, the culture/entertainment sector, the tourism sector and the IT sector.

9 For the initial development, building on the strength of SoHo to establish a vertical mixed-use program catered to tourist and local alike. Drawing from culture and entertainment program, establishing institutions with strong emphasis on art and cultural and other similar elements presently lacking in Hong Kong. These could include landscape parks, art house cinemas; contemporary/new art and media art galleries; food and beverage establishments, boutique hotels, and community facilities including a community center with a museum of local history and a library, inter-mixed with various residential-office-studio buildings catering to the IT industry.

10 The subsequent phases of programming and development should be devised with more ambiguity, in an attempt to absorb cultural, social and heritage variables of the area, encouraging tactical improvisations by current and future inhabitants and to map out future extensions and linkages with other entertainment hubs in the Central District.

Progressive porosity

The proposal of the new line is intended as a critique and an elaboration of the existing escalator plan. Infusing the original goals with urbanistic strategies, detailed considerations of movement patterns, social and physical structure, site characteristics to form a comprehensive plan without reliance on current successes, future accidents, chances and speculation.

The new line emphasizes the relationship between machine infrastructure and urban context. It produces progressive porosity through the intersection of mechanical infrastructure and the flow of people, the changing pace and terrain, and the interchanges where the discharging, filtering and looping motion merge to create the next city.

Figs. 8 and 9. SoHo Escalator

GROUND ZERO: THE REBUILDING OF A CITY

ALEXANDER GARVIN

What about pluralist democracy? Americans have been struggling with this question since the birth of our republic. Alexander Hamilton asked in *Federalist Paper* no. 1 whether we are "really capable" of "establishing good government" through "*reflection and choice*, or... forever destined" to make political decisions by "*accident and force*." Our efforts to rebuild Lower Manhattan during the first 24 months following 9/11 demonstrate resoundingly that the answer is "reflection and choice."

Who is in charge?

There is considerable confusion about who is in charge of rebuilding Lower Manhattan because it involves so very many players. In our market-driven, government-regulated economy the property owners are not alone in determining what will be built. The Port Authority of New York and New Jersey, a bi-state agency formed in the early 1920s, owns the largest part of the site. The Metropolitan Transportation Authority (MTA), a public-benefit corporation chartered by the New York Legislature State in 1965, owns and operates two subway lines that pass through the site. The N.Y. State Department of Transportation owns and operates the state highway, known as West Street, on the western edge of the World Trade Center. The City of New York owns the other streets that bound the property as well as portions of the site itself and rights-of-way within it. Across West Street is Battery Park City, owned by another Authority created in 1968 by the New York State Legislature. It leases the World Financial Center, an 8,000,000 square foot complex of office buildings designed by Cesar Pelli, to the Brookfield Properties Corporation, which also owns One Liberty Plaza, a 2.2 million square foot office building designed by Skidmore, Owings, and Merrill, across Church Street, the eastern boundary of the site. In between the World Financial Center and West Street lies the Hudson River Park, a five-mile long, 550-acre linear park stretching north to 59th Street. It is owned and operated by the Hudson River Park Trust, a city/state partnership created in 1998. Since the Governor of New York appoints the leadership of Port Authority, MTA, Battery Park City, the Hudson River Park Trust, and the LMDC, George Pataki had a particularly prominent role.

The Port Authority's leaseholders are no less important. Silverstein Properties, Inc., and Westfield America, Inc. had signed a 99-year lease to operate the World Trade Center just seven weeks before the attack. Westfield had the right to up to 600,000 square feet of retail space. Silverstein had the right to rebuild the office space. Marriott International, Inc., a worldwide hospitality company with more than 2,600 lodging properties, had rights to a hotel on the site. In addition the United States government leased office space for the U.S. Customs Service.

Then there are the insurance companies against whom these various property owners have claims and the lenders who provided the money; the victims of the attack, the families of the victims, the survivors, and the rescuers; the occupants of Lower Manhattan's former 2nd and 3rd class office buildings converted to residential use over the last decade, the residents of Battery Park City and Lower Manhattan's apartment buildings; the large and small businesses that provided white collar employment, small and large retailers; the people who live nearby in Chinatown, the Lower East Side, and Tribeca; and a wide array of public officials, community groups, and civic organizations.

Finally there is the government of the City of New York. It had been in conflict with the Port Authority for decades because its leaders, particularly Rudolph Giuliani, believed it was not providing the city with the money to which it was entitled. The City had been demanding a fair payment in lieu of taxes that similar privately-owned property would have paid on a site as large as the World Trade Center. It also believed that the Port Authority was not paying adequate rent to the city pursuant to its lease on La Guardia and Kennedy Airports. More important, Port Authority bureaucrats routinely ignored City agencies. They in turn resented Port Authority arrogance. Most important, virtually every city official, from Mayor Michael Bloomberg on down, resented the fact that they had no say in anything the Port Authority did.

Step 1: generating consensus

Governor George Pataki and Mayor Rudolph Giuliani created the Lower Manhattan Development Corporation (LMDC) to supervise rebuilding. Its most important task was to bring these players together within a workable decision-making process. Too often, bringing together so many powerful players results in gridlock.

The LMDC used a combination of traditional techniques in untraditional ways to involve the critical players: press releases, advisory councils, public hearings, and exhibitions. Traditional participation strategies were insufficiently inclusive and only permitted people to react to what was happening.

From the beginning the LMDC worked hard to involve a broader range of participants. It created eight advisory councils to deal separately with concerns of 1) victims families; 2) the real estate industry; 3) arts, education, and tourism; 4) financial services businesses; 5) professional firms; 6) residents; 7) restaurants, retailers and small business; and 8) transportation and commuters. In addition it established a "General Advisory Council" of public officials. Members of the board of directors of the LMDC had been meeting regularly with these councils. As soon I joined the LMDC as vice president for planning, design, and development, I began making presentations to the councils. After the first few meetings, I came to understand that the councils were little more than forums to hear about what was happening and express frustration over the slow pace of reconstruction.

I gathered the result of these talks into a set of principles. These principles, put together with Hugh Eastwood and Chris Glaisek became the *Principles & Preliminary Blueprint for the Future of Lower Manhattan*, which the LMDC issued on April 2nd. Publication allowed the LMDC to use a second traditional form of public participation: the public hearing.

Step 2: the public hearing

The LMDC's first public hearing, facilitated by Carolyn Lukensmeyer of America Speaks, was held on May 2nd at Pace University in Lower Manhattan. More than a thousand people attended. For the first time, opinions other than victims' families, local leaders, and the Port Authority were being presented very forcefully. Among the most assertive were people who wanted the towers back, who demanded investment in Chinatown and the Lower East Side, and who had specific designs to present. Two important considerations emerged that had been overlooked in the original *Principles*: 1) universal access (for the disabled), and 2) security (including protection of building mechanical systems from chemical and biological terrorism). More important, people clearly said they did not want *just anything* erected on the site. One particularly moving speaker explained that he had escaped from the World Trade Center's 79th floor before it collapsed. He had one simple request. "Please, make it the 7th wonder of the modern world."

I anticipated speakers who wanted their skyline restored. For months, proponents of minimum-resistance had been insisting on "financeable" 50-story office buildings, as if there were not other structures that could mark the skyline.

This public hearing was vital because, for the first time, ordinary city residents had an opportunity to influence what was happening. From that point on the press began to report opinions that previously had been ignored.

Step 3: public exhibition

Another way the LMDC was able to broaden involvement was through the use of public exhibitions. In July, after releasing the first six schemes, we opened an exhibition at Federal Hall in Lower Manhattan. It would be the first of several such exhibitions. Initial attendance was excellent. Once the press revealed the extent of dissatisfaction with these designs, attendance dropped off. All in all 17,000 visitors came to Federal Hall.

The second exhibition, which presented nine innovative designs at the Winter Garden at Battery Park City, was far more effective. There was more space for the show. The materials displayed were very much more impressive: models, video presentations, and huge illustrative drawings. Some of the designers (particularly those with international reputations) were very skillful at gaining public attention. The press hyped public interest by speculating on the likely "winner." More important, the designs themselves were popular. During the six weeks this show was open, more than 100,000 visitors came to see the designs.

Step 4: media and technology

Building true consensus required activities that made use of mass media and 21st-century technology. From the moment the first plane struck the World Trade Center, the press covered anything and everything that had to do with Lower

Manhattan. Each of New York's five daily newspapers assigned at least one full-time reporter to the story. There was something on television virtually every day. Monthly meetings of the LMDC board of directors were routinely televised and reported on in print the next day. Every time we released proposals for the site of the World Trade Center, newspapers, magazines, and TV stations ran polls to determine the favorites.

An important way to involve the public, therefore, was to make sure the press was always adequately informed, which would in turn report to the public. The LMDC press relations were the responsibility of Matt Higgins, vice president for communications. Before joining LMDC, he had served as press secretary to Mayor Rudolph W. Giuliani. In that capacity he had come to know many of the journalists covering Lower Manhattan as well as how to get them to report favorably on what was happening. Higgins spent much of his day on the phone spinning the stories that would appear in the papers or on television.

Readership and ratings have a marked effect on the way in which high profile projects like this one are represented, and the press concentrated on a limited number of players who provided colorful material for their stories. They reported on victims' families who were upset about real or imagined attempts to place anything on the "sacred ground" where loved ones had been murdered, individuals with property rights who complained about real or imagined attempts to keep them from recouping the full value of their investments, and government officials who objected to real or imagined actions excluding them from the decision-making process.

Computer technology allowed the LMDC to open up the decision-making process using its website, *Listening to the City* (a computerized 21st-century version of a town meeting developed by America Speaks), and the results of computerized polling by the media. In April, the LMDC established a web site.[1] It allowed a wide range people who had not been to the public hearing to comment on the *Principles & Blueprint*. More important, it provided a mechanism for LMDC staff to assess the extent and range of opinions, rather than just react to the few opinions covered by the press.

The website proved to be an extremely effective way of getting the public to participate. In July 2002, when the LMDC released the initial six designs for the site, there were over 700,000 hits on the website, 570,000 of whom visited the site only once. For the first time, urban design and planning were the subject of computerized national polls. *The New York Post* ran a poll with over 150,000 respondents. CNN had a poll with 200,000. During the six weeks following the December release of the nine innovative designs there were 7 million hits on the website, 2 million of which visited the site only once.

The second application of computer technology was the work of America Speaks. February 7, 2002, the Civic Alliance to Rebuild Downtown New York (an ad hoc coalition of more than 85 organizations) brought together 650 people to discuss the future of Lower Manhattan. It hired America Speaks to organize and run this contemporary version of an old-fashioned town meeting. Louis Tomson, the recently appointed president of the LMDC, attended the event. He was so impressed that he decided to hold a similar event when the LMDC presented its first six schemes for rebuilding the World Trade Center. Tomson asked the Civic Alliance and America Speaks to work with the LMDC to organize the event and persuaded the Port Authority to join with the LMDC in providing most of the money to pay for the event.

New York City has a long history of public participation. Its 59 community boards and their committees hold public hearings all the time. The City Planning Commission and the City Council and its Committees hold hearings. The process, however, is entirely reactive. Speakers testifying can be questioned, but they cannot ask questions. It is a process that encourages advocates to bring a large number of participants who present repetitive testimony and grandstand. But it rarely provides a great deal of useful commentary.

Computer technology made interactive participation possible. As America Speaks demonstrated, it is now possible to bring together large numbers of people to participate in face-to-face deliberation, even in a sprawling metro-politan region.

We had to find a way to prevent any particular interest group from dominating the July 20th *Listening to the City* event. This was achieved by using the press and the LMDC website to announce to millions of New Yorkers that the event would be held at the Javits Convention Center. Those who wished to participate had to fill out registration forms. When the 4,300 participants arrived they were assigned to tables seating twelve people in a manner that insured diversity and precluded domination by any particular interest or demographic group.

Each table had a volunteer facilitator, electronic keypads, and wireless connections to a central computer network. The central staff included a "theme

—— 1
<http://www.renewnyc.com>.

team" that read and distilled key ideas from each table and a "tabulating team" that sorted demographic information, reactions to key ideas, and responses to specific questions. Large video screens projected this material throughout the hall. Consequently, participants had visible evidence that they and their opinions were part the process. They were able to compare their positions with those of the group as a whole. Computer tabulation allowed the LMDC to see how different demographic and interest groups responded.

Never before had so many people participated in a discussion of planning, urban design, or downtown redevelopment. Rather than asking the public to comment of decided-upon plans, the LMDC presented alternatives and asked for their opinion. It was unequivocally told to come up with better alternatives.

Creating a 21st-century business district

I believed that neither reconstructing the "historical" street grid nor creating a 20th-century superblock could transform Lower Manhattan into a 21st-century downtown. Yamasaki's superblock had caused problems: blocking pedestrian and vehicular traffic and drawing people away from city streets to its underground shopping mall.

There was no one exact street grid to be restored. At the beginning of the 18th century the Hudson River edge of Manhattan Island was at Greenwich Street. Church Street stopped at Liberty Street and resumed its course north of what is today Vesey Street. At the beginning of the 19th century the island had been filled in as far as Washington Street. By the beginning of the 20th century, heavily trafficked piers reached out from West Street, now the island's water edge, into the Hudson River. By the time the Twin Towers were destroyed, the piers had been demolished and the coastline had been filled in to make way for Battery Park City.

After 9/11 we had to reconcile 21st-century demands for a pedestrian-friendly public realm with the existing configuration of downtown streets crowded with cars, buses, and trucks making their way through the narrow, skyscraper-lined canyons of Lower Manhattan.

That 21st-century site plan also had to tie together the Path rail system with city subway lines. It had to create a grand place of arrival and departure for tens of thousands of commuters who would once again pour in and out of the World Trade Center. The resulting street pattern had to create sites for the Port Authority's leaseholders to build marketable office buildings, retail stores, and hotel facilities. Perhaps most difficult of all, the heart of the nation's third largest downtown had to grow back around a memorial appropriate to the events of 9/11.

The LMDC began by hiring Peterson/Littenberg Architecture and Urban Design. Peterson/Littenberg was selected because it was particularly familiar with the area. In 1994, working for the Battery Park City Authority, the firm had prepared a master plan for all of Lower Manhattan that won the PA (*Progressive Architecture Magazine*) design award. Over the next three months they examined a range of alternatives including orthogonal grids, diagonal grids, and large blocks with and without structures where the Twin Towers had stood.

In May, Beyer Blinder Belle joined the search for a suitable site plan. The firm was known for urban design and restoration. It had been responsible for the renovation of Grand Central Terminal and Ellis Island. Under the leadership of Jack Beyer, it examined alternatives that precluded erecting any buildings on the footprints of the Twin Towers.

When the Port Authority and the LMDC decided to present concept plans to the public, both firms presented a large selection to choose from. They decided to show four schemes by Beyer, Blinder and Belle that left the footprints unbuilt and two by Peterson/Littenberg that did not. Both agencies explained that these six schemes were "concept plans" intended to "illustrate ideas for land use, infrastructure planning and building massing... not architectural designs for proposed buildings."

The public thought the six concept plans were genuine development proposals. In fact, they only illustrated different approaches to the site. There was general agreement on the need for something better. People wanted their skyline back. They wanted a street grid (rather than the 16-acre superblock that had stood on the site) and a variety of open spaces of different sizes (rather than one large windswept plaza). They wanted a suitable memorial to the events of September 11th. They wanted the redevelopment plan to treat the footprints of the twin towers with respect. Only one element among the six designs had widespread support: transforming the state highway, known as West Street, into a grand boulevard as proposed in the "Memorial Promenade" scheme prepared by Peterson/Littenberg.

The leadership of the LMDC decided that the only way to obtain better results was to open the process to the world's most imaginative designers. It sought designers whose work demonstrated "risk-taking and inspiration" in order to produce "innovative designs." Respondents were told that this was "NOT a design competition" and would "not result in the selection of a final plan." Rather, the intent was "to generate creative and varied concepts to help plan the future of the site." I was convinced that the desired better results would not emerge if we employed conventional planning methods. We needed an innovative approach.

Conventional planning

The usual approach to redevelopment planning is to seek recommendations from "experts." September 11th generated a great deal of "expert" planning by famous designers who made unsolicited proposals. The Max Protetch Gallery exhibited and then published a book illustrating sixty such schemes by some of the world's most famous architects. Herbert Muschamp, architecture critic for the *New York Times* commissioned similar plans from some of his favorite designers for an issue of its *Sunday Magazine*.

One designer proposed a handsome suspension bridge for pedestrians only, connecting New Jersey with the site of the World Trade Center. Another proposed transforming the entire site into memorial within which there were miniature twin towers listing the names of all the victims of the event. Many designers invented funky shapes for the world's tallest skyscraper. Virtually all these "experts" ignored the rights of the area's stakeholders, the needs of potential building tenants, the sources of financing for any construction, and the messy conflicts among the players in Lower Manhattan.

More conventional forms of "expert" planning involve real clients. The client might be a government agency that commissions feasibility studies. It might hire a planning, architecture, or landscape architecture firm to prepare a redevelopment plan. Sometimes, it simply sells land to (expert) real estate developers letting them determine the right thing to do. Like police roundups in the movie *Casablanca*, the usual suspects are rounded up, producing the usual results. The public and the LMDC wanted something extraordinary.

Environmental laws usually require experts to study the impacts of alternative plans and then disclose of them in a public document. Unfortunately, these alternatives are examined after a plan has been decided on. Impact studies have become a big business. Development agencies spend millions of dollars paying for work produced by the firms that do the analyses. Thereafter, proponents and opponents spend millions more on litigation. Thus, rather than fostering decisions by "reflection and choice," environmental reviews tend to become litigation protection devices.

Sometimes a community will invite a panel of "expert" visitors. Often it will bring them to certify already agreed-upon projects *or* to stop them. Expert panels often make effective recommendations. The Urban Land Institute, for example, organized and administered the expert panel that recommended the location for Denver's Coors Field.

A currently popular version of this panel of experts is a "charrette" that brings the experts together with the public. Contemporary charrettes consist of meetings (usually extending over several days) at which the participants discover and explore ideas. The ideas are discussed in the presence of invited experts and community residents. Once the ideas have gained some acceptance among the participants, expert designers develop site plans and sketch proposals for specific locations. This requires a large enough staff of architects to prepare initial designs. Once accepted, the resulting plan establishes an appropriate context for future development and may be used to explore the physical and financial feasibility of their recommendations.

The firm of Duany/Plater-Zyberk (DPZ) is probably the most effective practitioner of planning by charrette. Its charrettes work well in smaller communities where fewer players are involved with planning for lower density sites. Planning at a larger scale for major cities requires greater technological sophistication and more complex roles for the major participants.

Public officials usually are leery of proceeding without public consensus. In an effort to obtain public support they schedule public hearings or attend community meetings. Such events help them to determine what interested parties would like. The problem with this approach is that, unlike experts, most citizens do not have the professional training to assess what structures can be accommodated on a particular site, how much market demand there is for a particular use, how much money can be raised to finance the project and where that money can be obtained, or what would be involved in executing a particular proposal. Ordinary citizens, however, easily recognize bad ideas. The trick is to provide them with as much information as possible and devise appropriate, democratic mechanisms for them to express opinions that reflect this information.

Government employees are rarely ready to let the public decide what to do. They prefer to seek consensus among reigning bureaucrats, Too often, the people that implement these plans have not participated in the decision-making process and have to alter the plans significantly to meet the realities of the situation.

Innovative Design Process

In the aftermath of *Listening to the City*, the LMDC decided to jettison 20th-century approaches to planning. I sought help from New York New Visions, a civic coalition of 21 architecture, engineering, planning, and design organizations that had been formed in the wake of events of September 11th. Together we developed the ideas that the LMDC called the Innovative Design Process.

At the insistence of LMDC board members Roland Betts and Billie Tsien, we decided to proceed independent of the Port Authority. More important, we decided against holding a competition for a scheme that would be executed as designed. New York New Visions contributed much of the substance and the language of a *Request for Qualifications* (*RFQ*).[2] Respondents were asked to submit "work samples of past architecture, urban design, planning, and development projects" that demonstrated "risk-taking and inspiration."

On the first page the *RFQ* announced in bold type: "This is NOT a design competition and will not result in the selection of a final plan. It is intended to generate creative and varied concepts to help plan the future of the site." Nevertheless, the press, the design community, and, consequently, the public thought LMDC wanted winners and losers, rather than ideas from "the most talented and creative designers to aid in envisioning the future of the World Trade Center site."

The *RFQ* was issued August 19, 2002.

Once again I sought help from New York New Visions. It recommended that the finalists be selected by a panel of professionals not connected with LMDC and submitted lists of potential panelists that included: architects, landscape architects, planners, and representatives of cultural institutions. New York New Visions recommended that the group include an architect from outside the United States. Unfortunately, although each international architect selected did agree to serve, none was physically able to attend.

Submissions came in from every continent except Antarctica. Altogether, over 400 teams responded.

Once the LMDC announced the participants in the innovative design study, the Port Authority and virtually every city and state agency wanted to join the process. This was essential because the information needed to prepare initial designs had to come from the Port Authority, which owned the site. More important, any participating agency would be inclined to accept and build whatever resulted from the innovative design study.

October 11th, nearly a hundred participants crowded into the LMDC conference room for an all-day introduction to the innovative design study. The design teams included: 1) Studio Daniel Libeskind; 2) Foster and Partners; 3) Richard Meier, Peter Eisenman, Charles Gwathmey & Steven Holl; 4) THINK (Rafael Vinoly, Frederic Schwartz, Ken Smith, and Shigeru Ban); 5) United Architects (Greg Lynn, Reiser & Umemoto, and Kevin Kennon); 6) Peterson/Littenberg; and 7) Skidmore, Owings and Merrill leading a team of artists and architects from around the world.

Representatives of President Bush, Governor Pataki, Mayor Bloomberg, the LMDC, the Port Authority, the New York State Department of Transportation, the Metropolitan Transportation Authority (MTA), and the New York City Department of Transportation presented material about the site and the issues that needed to be addressed. Each team was given a thick portfolio containing a specific program, a planning context for all of Lower Manhattan that included actions the city and the LMDC recommended, a computer disc with digital drawings of the site with specific measurements, and a variety of relevant reports that had been issued by the LMDC, the Port Authority, city and state agencies.

Thereafter, every two weeks the staff of the LMDC and the Port Authority met separately with each design team. These sessions were informal and lasted about two hours. Each team presented their ideas and, as its proposals crystallized, a range of possible designs. They asked questions of the LMDC and Port Authority staff, which was often able to provide technical support, and invariably had questions and reactions of their own.

— **2**
A *Request for Qualifications* (*RFQ*) asks only for the qualifications of the firms offering their services. A *Request for Proposals* (*RFP*) also asks for a presentation of how those firms will go about their work, how long it will take, who will do the work, and how much it will cost.

United Architects, Meier-Eisenman-Gwathmey-Holl, Foster and Partners, and Peterson/Littenberg spent considerable time working out underground connections between the Path commuter rail system, subway lines, truck servicing, parking for buses and black cars, and surrounding properties. The designers were asked to propose how the city could grow around the memorial, to indicate how people would come to and leave the memorial, and to set aside specific territory that would be the setting for the memorial design that would emerge later from a design competition. Some solutions were polar opposites. Foster and United Architects both proposed ramps leading underground to the footprints of the twin towers. Foster's solution treated the footprints as sacred territory. Visitors could walk around them and look into rectangular volume of space formed by walls that continued high enough to preclude seeing anything but the results of the competition, in particular the world's tallest tower, which he proposed to build across the street. United Architects insisted that visitors walk on the footprints and look up to see tall buildings that enveloped the site of the memorial in a manner similar to a forest of sequoia trees. Studio Libeskind and Peterson/Littenberg both proposed to keep the memorial below grade, but open to the sky. Libeskind left the foundation walls exposed in memory of the event. Peterson/Littenberg proposed to heal the gash by creating a quiet contemplative garden on the site.

The seven teams made their final presentations on December 16th and 17th to the Steering Committee, consisting of Diana Taylor (representing Governor Pataki); Daniel Doctoroff (representing Mayor Bloomberg); Anthony J. Sartor, Anthony Kushner, Joseph Seymour (representing the Port Authority); and John Whitehead, Roland Betts, and Louis Tomson (representing the LMDC), and a variety of board and staff members of the Port Authority and the LMDC. On the 18th each team presented their work to a press conference televised around the world.

The next day the LMDC opened an exhibition of drawings and models of all nine schemes at the Winter Garden in Battery Park City. All nine schemes designs also were displayed on the LMDC website, which had 2 million unique visitors (7 million hits) in the first two weeks following the press conference.

During the six weeks that followed the staff of the LMDC and the Port Authority analyzed all nine schemes. They worked with a variety of consultants on traffic, engineering, construction cost and marketability of office and retail proposals. They examined the designs for appropriateness of their memorial settings, compatibility with the program and the mayor's vision for Lower Manhattan, and practicability of their streets, blocks, and development parcels. They studied how well the site plan connected with surrounding districts and how successfully they phased development over time. The LMDC also tabulated the public response and evaluated the strength of public support for each scheme. Other than Norman Foster's twinned tower, which had a slight lead in popularity, the professional analysis coincided with public support.

February 4th, the LMDC and the Port Authority announced that they would work with THINK on its proposal for a "World Cultural Center" (The Twin Towers of Culture) and Studio Libeskind on the proposal it called "Memory Foundations." For the next three and a half weeks each team altered their design to deal with problems that had surfaced during the LMDC–Port Authority review.

THINK redesigned the tower foundations so that they would not interfere with the Path trains running underneath. In order to reduce the cost of the towers, it also reduced the diameter and height of each tower and altered its structure. In order to permit large numbers of people onto the site, the huge reflecting pool and bridge overpasses were replaced by a paved open spaces directly accessible from surrounding streets. The continuous pedestrian underpass along the length of Greenwich Street was eliminated because it would have required creating a support structure for the subway (which had been built as a slab on grade) running beneath the street. In order to provide more practical development sites, the team redesigned the street grid east of Greenwich Street.

Studio Libeskind's plan had different structural difficulties. The slurry wall required several floors for lateral stability and needed to be protected from the weather. The 1776 tower became more of a TV antenna and less of a vertical garden. The elevated walkway encircling the site was eliminated. As in the THINK scheme, the office building and retail sites were made more commercially attractive.

Libeskind also replaced the triangular open spaces on the right-of-way Cortlandt Street, between Church and Greenwich Streets, with a glass-covered, pedestrian galleria. Most important, the railroad station was reoriented to open onto the proposed new main square of Lower Manhattan, which he calls the "Wedge of Light," and the tower that had been on the south side of the square was eliminated, opening up this grand public square to the sun.

A 21st-century planning process

On February 27, at an internationally televised press conference Governor Pataki and Mayor Bloomberg announced that they had decided to proceed with the Libeskind scheme – a scheme, which was acceptable to the players whose approval was necessary for anything to go forward. Its poetic evocations of the "Freedom Tower" set against the Statue of Liberty, "Wedge of Light," and exposed slurry wall that emerged from the Innovative Design Process resonated with the public. It was centered around a grand piazza enclosed by a railroad station, a memorial and museum, a performing arts center, and a convention hotel. This piazza would give the canyons of Lower Manhattan what most cities possessed: a main square. It did so by making the intersection of Greenwich and Fulton Streets the most desirable location downtown.

A great many people believed that the design was complete and construction could begin immediately. There isn't an architect alive who can design and prepare construction documents for an entire downtown district in the few weeks that had been available. Over the months and years to come the plan will be altered again and again and again.

The planning process that resulted in the selection of the Libeskind design is as important as the design itself. It established an interactive process in which design played a primary role, but in which the designer had to work with and satisfy the other participants in the planning game. It also established a mechanism for the public to affect the outcome of the planning process. Most important, it brought together key decision-makers and provided them with the information with which to make intelligent choices.

The two-month interactive process was unlike any conventional planning process. The LMDC cast a wide net to find designers whom it asked to conceive realistic development strategies. The design teams that were selected were not asked to imagine any future for the World Trade Center. They were given a detailed city planning agenda to satisfy. Nor were they left to design in a vacuum. They met for two hours every two weeks with representatives of the LMDC, the Port Authority, and other players. This interaction kept many of the participants from conceiving the unrealistic projects that frequently emerge from design competitions.

Computer technology and satellite television made possible a level of public participation that could not have been imagined during most of the 20th century. Digitalized images created by some of the world's great architects were made available to television viewers and internet users everywhere. For the first time, there was a planning process in which widespread citizen participation was unavoidable.

The two finalists were not selected on the basis of the images they presented. The LMDC and the Port Authority hired consultants who worked with their staffs to evaluate the parcelization and street pattern, traffic flow, marketability, constructability, development cost, phasing, memorial setting, and public reaction to each scheme. The results of that six-week analysis were presented to a Steering Committee that had been established to decide on the future of the site. Its decision was unanimous.

Lower Manhattan has been evolving much the way I think that the American Constitution evolved: out of the realties of the situation and the tug of war among very, very disparate interests. We were able to involve a particularly large, contentious, and powerful set of players in a new approach to planning that none of them could control. The result was agreement on an innovative design by one of the world's great architects. What had been an initial disaster was transformed into a consensus and a site plan that most participants were ready to accept.

Not everybody liked or voted for the Libeskind plan, just as not everybody liked or voted for the Constitution. But a large enough consensus came together to adopt it. As was the case with the Constitution, each of the parties involved in the future of Lower Manhattan has in mind a quite different idea of what consensus means and how to implement it. The job ahead for all New Yorkers is to see that the inevitable changes that will be made are the result of "*reflection and choice*, rather than "*accident and force*." If, as I believe, we will succeed in creating a great downtown, we will in the process have set forth an effective, new model for planning in a market-driven, pluralistic democracy.

The city is adjourned

Roger Connah is a writer, researcher and architectural historian based in Stockholm, and Ruthin, North Wales, where he runs the Hotel Architecture, a small guest house for discerning readers and malt whisky fanciers. Some of his many books include the award-winning *Writing Architecture: Fragments, Fantomas, Fictions*; *Welcome to the Hotel Architecture*; *How Architecture Got Its Hump*; *Aaltomania*; *Grace and Architecture*; *Sa(l)vaged Modernism*; and *Zahoor ul Akhlaq*. His films include *Take Five*; *27 Minute Lies*; *Drive*; and *Aaltomania*. Recently he has been visiting professor at the University of Texas School of Architecture in Arlington. He is currently at work on *Modernism, an Architectural Narrative* (Finland); *The House for De Kooning's Friend* (text and photographs); and *The Collected Works of Zahoor ul Akhlaq*.

Peggy Deamer is associate dean and associate professor at the Yale School of Architecture. Ms. Deamer is a principal in the firm of Deamer + Phillips, whose projects have been featured in various publications. The firm received a New York AIA Interiors Award and was one of the 1993 Urban League of New York "Emerging Voices." The firm's Stetson University Center in Celebration, Florida, was recently completed, and received an Honor Award from the Tampa Bay AIA. Articles by Ms. Deamer have appeared in *Assemblage*; *Architecture and Body*; *Thinking the Present*; and *Drawing/Building/Text*. She received a B.A. from Oberlin College, a B.Arch. from Cooper Union, and an M.A. and a Ph.D. from Princeton University.

Neil Denari is an architect, educator, and principal of Neil M. Denari Architects, Inc., in Los Angeles, California. Since 1988, the office has been engaged in design projects on many different scales for a variety of international locations. Mr. Denari has taught at the Department of Architecture and Urban Design at UCLA since 2002, where he is to be appointed to the position of studio professor. From 1997 to 2001, he was the director of the Southern California Institute of Architecture (SCI-Arc). In 2002, he was given both the Richard Recchia Award and the Samuel F. B. Morse Medal for architecture from the National Academy of Design in New York for distinguished work in the field. Mr. Denari is the author of two bestselling books, *Interrupted Projections* (1996) and *Gyroscopic Horizons* (1999). He has exhibited his work widely and lectured internationally for the last 20 years.

Joy Garnett is a painter based in New York City whose paintings are made from found photographs. Her sources range from declassified government documents to images from mass media and news wires. She has recently been awarded an artist grant from the Anonymous Was A Woman Foundation. <http://www.firstpulseprojects.org>.

Alexander Garvin has combined a career in urban planning and real estate with teaching, architecture, and public service. He served as vice president for planning, design and development of the Lower Manhattan Development Corporation. He is currently managing director of planning of NYC2012, the committee to bring the Summer Olympics to New York City in 2012. From 1970 to 1980 he held prominent positions in New York City government, including deputy commissioner of housing and director of comprehensive planning. Mr. Garvin is a member of the National Advisory Council of the Trust for Public Land, on the board of directors of the Society of American City and Regional Planning History, and a fellow of the Urban Land Institute. He is the author of *The American City: What Works, What Doesn't*, winner of the 1996 American Institute of Architects book award in urbanism, and one of the principal authors of *Urban Parks and Open Space*. In April 2001, the American Planning Association released his latest book, *Parks, Recreation, and Open Space: A 21st-Century Agenda*. He earned his B.A., M.Arch., and M.U.S. from Yale University.

Zvi Hecker studied architecture at the Krakow Polytechnic (1949–1950) and at the Technion, the Israeli Institute of Technology in Haifa (1950–1954), where he received his degree in engineering and architecture in 1955. He also studied painting at the Avni Academy of Art in Tel Aviv (1955–1957). Following two years of military service in the Corps of Engineers of the Israeli Army, he set up a private practice in 1959, working with Eldar Sharon (until 1964) and with Alfred Neumann (until 1966). He is a visiting lecturer at numerous schools of architecture throughout Europe and the United States. His more recent projects include the Spiral Apartment House in Ramat Gan, the Jewish School in Berlin, the Palmach Museum of History in Tel Aviv (with Rafi Segal), the Synagogue Memorial Lindenstrasse in Berlin (with Micha Ullman and Eyal Weizman), the Jewish Cultural Center in Duisburg, the Royal Dutch Military Police Campus in Schiphol Airport, Amsterdam. In 1991 Zvi Hecker represented Israel at the 5th Venice Biennale of Architecture, and took part in the 6th, 7th and 9th Biennale of Architecture in Venice in 1996, 2000 and 2004.

Sandy Isenstadt Specializing in American architecture, Mr. Isenstadt has written on postwar reformulations of modernism by Richard Neutra and Josep Lluis Sert; visual polemics in the urban proposals of Leon Krier and Rem Koolhaas; the history of refrigerator design, picture windows, real estate appraisal; and the fate of architectural memory in an information age. He is currently completing a book for Cambridge University Press on the historical development of a concept of "spaciousness" in American house and interior design, landscape architecture and planning, real estate, and land management. He teaches modern architectural history at Yale University.

C. J. Kang is a Korean-born, Japanese-raised artist. His work confronts cultural issues and questions preconditioned notions of boundary. He lives and works in Los Angeles. <http://www.geocities.com/chungmokang/>.

Leslie Lu is the chairman of the faculty board of architecture and an associate professor at the University of Hong Kong. Mr. Lu received his M.Arch. degree from Yale University, and was the recipient of the Monbusho Scholarship from the

Japan Ministry of Culture. He practiced professionally in the United States with Cesar Pelli and Associates, Hardy Holzman Pffifer Associates, Perkins Eastman Architects, Kohn Pedersen Fox Associates, and worked with Shinohara Kazuo on the design of the Centennial Hall, Tokyo Institute of Technology, Japan. Mr. Lu lectured and taught internationally, and served as visiting professor, lecturer and design critic in major universities including Cambridge University, CUHK, Chu Hai College, Columbia University, TU Delft, Princeton University, Shenzhen University, Tongji University, Tokyo Institute of Technology, Tsinghua University and Yale University. His writings and designs were published in international journals with translations in Chinese, Korean, Spanish and Japanese. He has recently completed a research project commissioned by the HK SAR Arts Development Council entitled "A Feasibility Study on Setting up a Visual Arts Academy in Hong Kong." His design of a contemporary fine arts gallery received the 2002 AIA/HK Honor Awards.

William McDonough is an internationally renowned designer and one of the primary proponents and shapers of what he and his partners call "the Next Industrial Revolution." *Time* recognized him as a "Hero for the Planet" in 1999, stating that "his utopianism is grounded in a unified philosophy that – in demonstrable and practical ways – is changing the design of the world." A leader in the sustainable development movement since 1977, Mr. McDonough helped launch the 'green office' movement in the U.S. with his design for the Environmental Defense Fund Headquarters, completed in 1985. His ideas and efforts were honored in 1996 when he became the first and only individual to receive the Presidential Award for Sustainable Development, the nation's highest environmental honor.

Richard Olcott is a design partner in Polshek Partnership Architects. He has been a member of the firm since 1979. Among Mr. Olcott's current designs are the WGBH Headquarters, the Omaha Performing Arts Center and the renovation, and expansion of the Yale University Art Gallery. Recent projects include Judy and Arthur Zankel Hall at Carnegie Hall, Oklahoma City Civic Center Music Hall, Iris and B. Gerald Cantor Center for Visual Arts at Stanford University, Seamen's Church Institute, and the *New York Times* Printing Plant. Since 1996, Mr. Olcott has been a commissioner on the New York City Landmarks Preservation Commission. He received a B.Arch. degree from Cornell University in 1979. Mr. Olcott is the recipient of the 2003–2004 Founders Rome Prize Fellowship awarded by the American Academy in Rome.

James Polshek is the founding partner in Polshek Partnership Architects. Among Mr. Polshek's current projects are the Vietnam Veteran's Memorial Education Center and the Newseum/Freedom Forum Foundation Headquarters. His recent buildings include Symphony Space, Scandinavia House, Rose Center for Earth and Space at the American Museum of Natural History, and the Santa Fe Opera. Mr. Polshek is a long time educator and served from 1972–1987 as

dean of the Columbia University Graduate School of Architecture, Planning and Preservation, where he co-founded the Temple Hoyne Buell Center for the Study of American Architecture. Mr. Polshek received a M.Arch. degree from Yale University in 1955, and in 1956 was a Fulbright Fellow at the Royal Academy of Fine Arts in Copenhagen.

Marjetica Potrc is a Ljubljana-based artist and architect. Her work has been featured in exhibitions throughout Europe and the Americas, including the Sao Paulo Biennial in Brazil (1996); *Skulptur. Projekte in Münster*, Germany (1997); Manifesta 3 in Ljubljana, Slovenia (2000); and *The Structure of Survival* at the Venice Biennale (2003); as well as in solo shows at the Guggenheim Museum in New York (2001); Künstlerhaus Bethanien in Berlin (2001); the Max Protetch Gallery, New York (2002); the Nordenhake Gallery in Berlin (2003); the PBICA in Lake Worth, Florida (2003); and the MIT List Visual Arts Center in Cambridge, Massachusetts (2004). In addition, Ms. Potrc has been the recipient of numerous awards, including grants from the Pollock-Krasner Foundation (1993 and 1999), a Philip Morris Kunstförderung Grant to participate in the International Studio Program of Künstlerhaus Bethanien in Berlin (2000), the Hugo Boss Prize 2000, Guggenheim Museum (2000), and a Caracas Case Project Fellowship from the Federal Cultural Foundation, Germany, and the Caracas Urban Think Tank, Venezuela (2002).

Evelyn Preuss is completing her doctoral thesis on East German film at Yale University, where she has been teaching German and film studies. She has published numerous articles on topics ranging from representational strategies and political theory in literature, the filmic politics of East German cinema and the intersection of identity, architecture and film aesthetics in recent German film. Her research interests encompass historical memory, identity politics and film and media theory.

Saskia Sassen is the Ralph Lewis Professor of Sociology at the University of Chicago, and Centennial Visiting Professor at the London School of Economics. Her most recent books are *Guests and Aliens* (1999) and the edited *Global Networks, Linked Cities* (2002). *The Global City* is out in a new, fully updated edition in 2001. She has also just completed for UNESCO a five-year project on sustainable human settlement for which she set up a network of researchers and activists in over 50 countries. Her books are translated into fourteen languages. She serves on several editorial boards and is an advisor to several international bodies. She is a member of the National Academy of Sciences Panel on Cities, a member of the Council on Foreign Relations, and chair of the new Information Technology, International Cooperation and Global Security Committee of the Social Science Research Council.

Rafi Segal received his professional degree (1993) and M.Sc. in Architecture (2001) from the Technion, the Israel Institute of Technology, Haifa. From 1992 to 2000 he worked together with architect Zvi Hecker on the design of the Palmach

History Museum built in Tel Aviv, and other projects. In 2000, he established his own practice in Tel Aviv dealing with research aside building, and also formed a partnership with architect Eyal Weizman. Their joint project *A Civilian Occupation: The Politics of Israeli Architecture* has been widely exhibited and reviewed. In fall 2003 Mr. Segal began undertaking a Ph.D. at Princeton University.

Mark C. Taylor is visiting professor of architecture and religion at Columbia University and the Cluett Professor of Humanities at Williams College. He received a *Doktorgrad* (Philosophy) from the University of Copenhagen in 1981, a Ph.D. from Harvard in 1973, and a B.A. from Wesleyan University in 1968. Mr. Taylor has written numerous books and essays on topics ranging from philosophy, theology and literature to art, architecture, technology and economics. His most recent books are: *The Moment of Complexity: Emerging Network Culture* (2001), *Grave Matters* (2002) and *Confidence Games: Money and Markets in a World without Redemption* (2004). Mr. Taylor has also produced an interactive CD-ROM, *Motel Réal: Las Vegas, Nevada*, and has mounted an exhibition at the Massachusetts Museum of Contemporary Arts (*Grave Matters*, 2002–3). His current multimedia projects include constructing a website, www.realfakes.org, and work with digital photography. Taylor has received many awards including the Distinguished Alumnus Award from Wesleyan University, the Carnegie Foundation for the Advancement of Teaching National College Professor of the Year award, the Rector's Medal from the University of Helsinki, and the American Academy of Religion Award for Excellence for his books *Nots* and *Altarity*.

Eyal Weizman is an architect and writer based in London. He is currently a professor of architecture at the Academy of Fine Arts in Vienna. Throughout his studies at the AA in London (1993–1998), he worked with Zvi Hecker in Berlin and did projects in partnership with him. He set up his private practice with Rafi Segal in 1999. Their projects included the rebuilding of the Ashdod Museum of Art (opened in June 2003), a stage-set for Itim Theatre Company (premiered at the Lincoln Centre in July 2003), a runner-up proposal for the Tel Aviv Museum competition and other projects. Together with the human-rights organization B'tselem, Mr. Weizman initiated a report on violations of human-rights and international humanitarian law through the use of architecture and planning titled "Land Grab." The map produced alongside this report was the first of its kind to represent the nature of planning and the formal dimension of the Israeli Occupation, and is currently widely used by international organizations. The exhibition and the publication *A Civilian Occupation: The Politics of Israeli Architecture*, which he edited/curated with Rafi Segal, was based on this human-rights research. These projects were banned by the Israeli Association of Architects, but later shown at the Storefront Gallery for Art and Architecture in New York (February 2003), in *Territories* at the Kunst-Werke Institute for Contemporary Art in Berlin (May 2003), and ever-updated versions of the ongoing project at the Witte de With Center for

Contemporary Art in Rotterdam (November 2003), at Berkeley University in San Francisco (March 2004), at the Konsthal in Malmö (May 2004), and at the Betzalel gallery in Tel Aviv. Eyal is now the editor of the series on Politics and Architecture in *Domus* magazine (Milan).

Michael Wesely and Lina Kim The *Brasilia* project is a cooperation between Lina Kim and Michael Wesely. Lina Kim was born in 1965 in Sao Paulo. Michael Wesely was born in 1963 in Munich. They live together in Berlin.